# Look! Up in the Sky!

## An Anthology of Comic Book Poetry

Edited by
**Ryk McIntyre, Melissa Guillet, Editor X**

Lay-out and Cover Design by
**Melissa Guillet**

Cover art by
**Kenneth McIntyre, Age 11
and his Dad**

Sacred Fools

Sacred Fools Press

**ISBN 978-0-6151-3764-3 pbk.**

Sacred Fools Press
215 River Avenue
Providence, RI 02908

Dedicated to
the Memory of Lisa King

# Table of Contents

## II. On Lisa King - Remembering a Heroic Life

## III. About Our Contributors

## IV. Acknowledgments

# Introduction:

## On Super Heroes & Lisa King

I 've never been that interested in super heroes that much. Even as a kid, I never got into the whole comic book/TV show/blockbuster movie thing. Super heroes, for the most part, bored me (the exception being Daredevil). The trouble, as I saw it, was that super heroes were so far removed from people I knew that I had no way to relate to them. They were too unreal to be even remotely believable. I spent most of my youth reading Peanuts anthologies. Now Charlie Brown was someone I could relate to. What really interested me were ordinary people with extraordinary talents, or those who had overcome extraordinary events. I was obsessed with Ripley's Believe It Or Not & the Guinness Book of World Records. I loved reading stories of people moving whole train engines or swallowing 14 swords or walking across a bed of hot coals. I was fascinated by people who hiked solo across Asia or held their breath underwater for seven minutes or who had lost their legs but climbed the Rocky Mountains on their hands. These were ordinary people who strove to do something beyond the normal and to a young boy growing up in a small town, that was something heroic.

I find it very appropriate that Lisa King drove the inspiration for this collection. Lisa was, to me, what a super hero should be. She possessed a great strength of spirit & will, could transform ordinary words into extraordinary poems with a flash of her pen, was able to leap boundaries & stereotypes in a single bound, all while remaining passionately human. But more importantly, Lisa had the ability to see the ordinary as something special. She knew that all of us have the same ability & she spent her life trying to show us through example. Lisa reminded all of us that we are extraordinary in one way or another, pointing out our shortcomings while always leaving us with hope. In a just and loving world, the comic book stores would be selling the latest issue of "The Adventures of the Amazing Lisa King" to waiting fans while the Superman & Captain America books gathered dust in the discount bin.

Taking a lesson from Lisa, the pieces in this collection strive to see super heroes in a new light. From the silly to the serious, the works here revisit what we take for granted so that we can view them from a new perspective. We may have lost Lisa too soon, but there is still so much we can learn from her. And if that isn't the sign of a true super hero, then I don't know what is.

Rest well, Lisa. You will always be a hero to us.

- Bill MacMillan, November 2006, Worcester, MA

Rev. Bill MacMillan is the founder of the Worcester Poetry Slam & Co-Founder of the Worcester Poets' Asylum. He Co-Hosted the 2005 iWPS and is a member of the Executive Council of Poetry Slam, Inc. Bill is also an accomplished visual artist & conservator.

# Foreword

## by Ryk McIntyre

I t all seemed like a good idea at the time. Of course, there are more than a few good-intention bricks on various roads that have that thought carved into their surfaces. And while the end result of all these many months of launching the anthology, then urging, pleading, guiding, threatening and otherwise talking people into submitting a poem, (let alone the construction of the beast) is something fundamentally different from where those roads lead to...well, it's been an enormous undertaking regardless.

The origin of this anthology gestated in several sources, but two of the key catylysts were hearing Dave MacPherson poem "Hench Men" at the Java Hut open mic in Worcester MA; and the Jim's Big Ego song "The Ballad Of Barry Allen." Both backed up the idea that comic book characters make great subjects for poems of all kinds, from the academic, as well as the performance spheres. Personally I love it when literature and Pop Culture combine, and have written more than my share of nerdy persona poems over the years.

For that fact, and other poetic sins, I wanted to make this a charity benefit. I got that idea from Lea Deschenes' "Where Your Mouth Is" performance series which she ran in Worcester, Mass. Each month she would combine spoken-word and music acts, and the proceeds went to a variety of deserving recipients. So I was ready to launch this project, as soon as I figured out which direction for the charity element to take.

Then I got the news back in February about Lisa King. And I knew. Of all the sad things that happened to Lisa over the years, one that stung most was that she was back in Boston for a while before she died and none of us even knew. Someone remarked that she feared she had been forgotten by the Poetry Scene. I know that wasn't true, and if this collection does anything, I'd be happiest if it helps keep her name on people's lips, her words in their heart, and the courage of her life as a high mark by which they can judge their own journey.

Lisa was a friend of mine through the 1980's and into the 90's. Then we lost touch and though I saw her a couple of times after that, I never got the time for a good one-on-one conversation about everything. Lisa, I'm sorry I lost touch with you. No one should ever have to feel forgotten.

This Anthology been a long, tiring, eye-straining, pain-in-the-everything business considering what it's taken to put it all together. If I had known at the beginning how much it would take, and will still take, to get this thing airborne and up there...well, I would've done it anyway. It seemed like a good idea at the time.

It still does.

# Bat Poem

Christopher Wood-Robbins

```
                         o         n
         silent ev      en     in        g flight
        a brief fl          icker of-        bat wings
       can be seen          darting t          hrough the
       jungle of towe      ring concre         te in pursuit
     of  a world-devour    ing evil - for     now, not only  the
   city,  but  also  the  caped  crusader's  legend  is at  stake. This
 fiend  the  Ivory  Ghoul,  a  towering  director  of corporate  mayhem,
 destroyed  Batman  by  changing  him  from  a  detective  to  a  pure ac-
 tion  hero.  If  he  can  tarnish  and  control  the  dark  knight's  im-
 age,  then  he  will  certainly  seize  and  extinguish  the  spark  of
 individual           creativity and enslave the           human race.
       You can  h       elp      fight this    dum         bing down
        by  writin      g        and  sp       e           aking your
          own  v                 oice                       here in
            this                 v                          enue.
```

# Look!  Up in the Sky!

# Volume I
Sylvia Bagaglio

In the beginning, there was Stan.
And Stan had Desk, and Desk sat empty.
And Stan said,
    Let there be Lamp!
And there was,
and Lamp had all the right springs and knobs and turny bits,
and it shone brightly on Desk.
And it was Just Dandy.
And Stan took stroll.
Stan returned, His legs freshly energized.
And Stan said,
    Let there be Pen and Paper, the one separated from the other!
And there was, and Pen was dark and Paper light,
so that there would be Contrast.
And it was Aces.
And Stan had a snack.
His hunger sated, Stan sat at Desk and picked up Pen.
And Stan said,
    Let there be Scene!
And Pen touched Paper, and Scene was created,
containing structures and streets,
fields and schools and automobiles,
and every Thing that hulketh therewith upon the page.
And it was Nifty.
And Stan went to wash the ink off His hands.
Newly cleansed, Stan returned to Desk, Pen, Paper, and Scene,
And Stan said,
    Let there be Exposition!
And Scene opened up to expose Situation,
a mostly happy time, but with a lurking, stealthy sense of foreboding.
And it was Definitely Cool.
And Stan went outside for some fresh air.
Full of Breath, Stan returned to Desk, so full of promise.
And Stan said,
    Let there be Villain!
And Pen and Paper revealed Villain,
and he was dark and shadowy,
full of Lurk and Sneak and Cross-hatching.
And he was Nasty.
And Stan went to get some coffee.
Now caffeinated, Stan sat again at Desk and Scene,
And Stan said,
    Let there be Hero, created in my image!
And Pen, Paper, Scene, Situation, and Villain all moved aside for Hero.
And Hero came to be, in the image of his maker;
he was full of Tall and Lean and Smart,
possessing of Trust and Strength and Wholesomeness,
keeper of Peace and Justice and Joy.
And he was Good.
And Stan kept right on working.
And Stan said,
    Let there be Action!

And Villain committed Dastardly Deeds,
setting a Trap for Hero,
And yea verily, Hero did fall for Villain's Trap,
because Hero was so full of Trust.
Trapped, Hero seemed unable to Thwart Villain...

Will Hero Thwart Villain? Can he outsmart the Evil Fiend? Shall he escape the Trap?
Find out in Volume II !

## The Heroes
Dennis Caswell

When word got out about Superman, especially the part
about how smartly Lois fills out a sweater, they began showing up
from every planet in cosmic tarnation:

the Man of Water, who can take any shape,
the Man of Smoke, who floats like hot snakes,
the Man of Rubber, rebounding off walls,
the Man of Stained Glass, reverent and lustrous,
the Man of Feathers, hopeful, always hopeful.

Whatever their powers, they all have the same need to use them,
to wait for the moment of utmost helplessness
before revealing themselves to be

the Man of Pudding, gooey and sweet, or
the Man of Leather, who smells good and wears well, or
the Man of Oatmeal, who's bland but helps you to purge, or
the Man of Bamboo, who you can't get rid of, or
the Man of Chalcedony, who possesses the power to intimidate
those who don't know what chalcedony is.

They've come to our planet in search of some evil to thwart,
some goodness to rescue, a place where their powers
are rare enough to be valuable.

There's probably one where you work, sitting through meetings
in silence, head down over the copier, disguised
as a Man of Earthly Concerns.

They're always disguised, these heroes. The only thing
they truly fear is the loss of their secret identities,
so they've studied our habits and learned

to live among us. You see them in the grocery store, pretending
to toy with a melon, when really they're maintaining vigilance:
ever alert for the cry of distress

that will send them bursting, chest first, out of their drab outerwear
to stand in spandex splendor and show the astonished earthlings
what heroes can be made of.

# It's a Bird!  It's a Plane!  It's Super-Manic Depressive Man!
Robert Dunn

When my Mom and Dad dumped me into that
Rocket ship, they cooed at me
"It's a new space age style cradle!"
And I believed them.
Figured I'd chill out, but then
The whole planet Clyfton exploded.

First I thought it was some cheap special effect
By the Trans Lux Luthor Animation Studios,
But when I didn't get any presents for my
First birthday—when I didn't even get
Taken out of the cradle—I knew
What side of the comet the tail was pinned on.
I didn't mind them saving my life, but Earth ...

Earth!

Didn't they read the briefing book on this place?

And the people!  Always needing rescuing
From runaway trains and alien invasions ...
Last time I brought this up, some smart alec said
I was an alien invasion.  I saw redder than my cape.
"Oh, yeah?  So who's going to rescue the world this time,
Mister Smartiepants Xenophobe?"  I politely inquired.
He told me.  (Har de har, that's gratitude for you.)

You and whose army?  I snorted.  Maybe you'd like to
Clip on the cape and save the world five times a week
And twice on Sunday.  His wife, bless her heart,
Gave him a warning kick under the table.  She's had her
Eye on me for some time now, but somehow, I just can't ...
Think her mascara reminds me of Clyftonite.
When I was growing up in Squallville, I wanted
To wear the eye mask and shoot silver bullets ...
We were so poor, the only silver we had was silverfish.
Now if I had it all to do over again, I'd have been
Bruce Sprayne ... It's not like that old fraud has
To work for a living.  And as for news casting, who
Needs it?  They put me on the Hollywood beat, for
Crying out loud, doing Barbara Walters style specials.
Last show I had to interview Christopher Reeve and
George Reeves and Christopher George and Christopher
Robin and Curious George and ... [phhfft!] ...
Never get a Pulitzer that way ...

## Meanwhile!
Alvin Lau

After a long day of saving the world, Clark Kent
gets cut off by the construction worker
he rescued from getting gooshed
by gigantic monster robots only hours before.

Deep breath, he reminds himself,
ignoring the lightning of nerves firing
across his back and the itch gnawing
under his thin blue tights.

That night, while playing on his computer,
Clark unleashes a zoo of disasters
onto the citizens of his made-up metropolis:

So lifelike, he admires how they trample
each other as they flee the tsunami,
how their lifeboats pop in rivers of lava,
how the missiles seem soft as toothpicks,
barely scratching the Super villain's skin

## Captain Ultimate and the Pelican of Doom
Tod Caviness

Your vaunted powers are useless here, Captain Ultimate!

I have ripped the redeemable box tops off your free reprieve from Life cereal, as it were. You may take my maniacal laughter for granted. Feel free to struggle for the amusement of my henchmen against your impregnable bonds as the pelican suspended above your head slowly eats through the bucket of herring, one of which contains a tablet of Alka-Seltzer that will cause the bird to explode, spattering your heroic cranium with a generous heaping of avian chum, the decomposition of which will breed maggots that will develop into flies destined to be caught in the flypaper hung from one end of these scales, eventually weighing it down enough to trip the switch tied to the other end of the scales that will activate the laser aimed squarely at your ever-so-quickly beating heart!

Life from death and death again from life: I'm sure even a straight-shooting Cartesian dualist like yourself can appreciate the irony. I can assure you, it's always no trouble to bring a bit of color into your grayscale world. Sometimes I pride myself in thinking that I have.

Still, I must admit a certain degree of nostalgia for the old days, without all these hidden agendas to our little contests. Remember the first time we did battle? I was working for Hitler back then, grafting monkey heads onto the severed necks of Jewish midgets. Still have no idea why. You broke into my laboratory without so much as a how-do-you-do, punched me in the nose, and sent me to jail.

Then, when I broke out years later I retrofitted my giant robot ostrich with a drill nose and went out to commandeer the world's oil supply. Would've been in good hands, I tend to think now, but no. You crushed my remote control unit, punched me in the nose and sent me to jail.

So I broke out and cut your hand off with a sword made from the Ultimate alloy that robs you of your powers, remember that? Oh, the look on your face, right before you punched me in the nose and sent me to jail.

Still, it was nothing compared to the reaction I got when I shot your girlfriend Mary Jane Stacy into the heart of the sun. Or the time I fed your parents their own kneecaps. Or when I sodomized Penultimate Lad with an umbrella before hanging him off the Sears Tower with his own intestines. Completely worth the trouble. By that time I had a cyborg nose anyway.

But you must see, that's always been your problem (and, perhaps, your salvation): you're so predictable, Captain. No wonder your comics sell like shit. You're always a step behind. Where I am the creative force, Shiva and Brahma all in one, you're ... well, you're not even in the pantheon, old boy. You're the garbage man.

Except that hasn't been the case lately, has it? I must have finally gotten to you. What's with this new black costume, the guns, the eye patch, the foul language, the -

... see, that's what I'm talking about right there. And no, Captain, fuck you, by the way. Or as you used to put it so much more eloquently, "Taste justice, evildoer!"

Where did we lose our way, eh? When did relevance slip away in the clamor of chin music and death ray explosions? There are no nefarious plots anymore, only full disclosure. Nobody takes the time anymore to construct a nice underwater deathtrap merry-go-round with electric bolo-shooting sea horses. There are only faceless snipers in the night and blameless burials in the morning. Nobody wants to rule the world anymore, my friend. They just want to own it.

Well. Toodle-pip, Captain Ultimate, for the last time. Can't say I won't miss you, in my way. Haven't told anyone but you, but I dare say I'll be hanging up the cowl and poison dart cane after tonight. Going to open a smoothie shop down by the park, maybe get a shih-tsu and a stair master for the underground lair. I hope you take comfort in that, and in the knowledge that the dance I perform on your grave will be as graceful and pointed as the one we used to do in those golden years, when each of us knew his ground and stood it.

And maybe, once a year or so, when there's nothing on television and the sleeping child of villainy stirs within my breast, I'll have a hooker dress up like you and punch me in the nose. For old times sake.

## The Last Laugh
Scott Woods

I told him,
> "I'll miss you when you're dead"
> a million times.

It was a joke; it's what I do.
It was always going to
> come down to this:
> one of us looking into lights
at the hand of the other.

We played at cowboys and indians
          but knew that one day
          there would be one too many
          corpses with smiles
          to make a joke about.
I saw it in his eyes, the breaking point.
He growled at me and
          laughter left my breast.

Money was never the object.
          and it was never just a game.
It was the prescription of a mad scientist,
          therapy for the mad offered by the mad.
We were never foes;
          always brothers.
Gotham's first sons,
          sick Siamese twins connected by
          grappling hooks and the stems of
          a million acid flowers.

Every April Fool's Day
          he would sneak into the asylum
          and we would trade knock knock jokes
          through the vents:

     Knock knock
                    Who's there?
     Batman.
                    Batman who?
     Batman and Robin, sittin' in a tree...

You'd think the world's greatest detective
          would be better at these things,
          but I kept him very busy some years.
There is no such thing as a perfectly
          bulletproof vest.
Any shot close enough to the heart
          will reach the heart.
I know: he's pierced mine
          over and over again
          for years.

Tonight,
          I lay a dozen carnations
          at his headstone.
And while eleven of them still held poison,
          one of them was filled
          with love.

## Madame Bat and Telekinesis Boy
Ratpack Slim

the story of how we met:
no one will ever believe.
there was this bank robbery occurring
it was the mcmanus gang
and they had the block locked down in a rain of gunfire and chaos.
the cops couldn't do squat.
and that's when you swooped in
and started kicking robber ass
well, more like glided, actually
with your beautiful bat wings
not some jet pack or miracle of science
but actual organic wings

your headgear reminded me a lot of a lucha libre mask
but it couldn't hide the fact that your eyes
were stunning
or that you had a great right hook

and i showed up
like i always do
floating on the air via mind power
hearing some bystander cry out
"look! it's telekinesis boy!"
as i gave them a sharp military salute and kept on a-floating

so we put the kibosh on the robbery together
me with my freakish mutant forehead
you with your leathery wings stretching from wrist to hip

between you whomping heinie like a hang glider from hell
and me yanking machine guns out of thugs' arms via mind-tongs
baby, we made a hell of a team.

and i always told myself
i would never date another super hero
way too much drama
you're always worried about super villain attacks
not to mention the paparazzi
and then there's the whole secret identity thing
(which the minute in-laws are involved is a major hassle)

and i did my best not to get swept up
in your awesome crime fighting technique
but even as precise and surgical as your aerial attacks were
i sensed a gentleness in you
that made my oversized noggin burst with giddy

after the arrests were made
and the photogs had snapped their aftermath shots
i asked your nom de plume
you said you didn't have one.

you wanted to call yourself bat-girl
it made perfect sense what with your wings and all
but copyright lawyers told you no effing way

(and this may be off-subject but
i couldn't get past the way your hair cascaded out from under your mask
or the cute way you called me "sir" with a smirk)

i suggested that you change your name to "the fallen angel"
that's me, though
it was the first thing that hit me
always thinking with my heart over my head
but you had a better sense of marketing than i did
(you said it sounded too apocalyptic)
and so we compromised on
madame bat

who knew that our first co-headline
the one that read
"telekinesis boy and madame bat thwart robbery"
would not be our last

i made good and damn sure that the next headline
referenced you first
it just sounded better
"madame bat and telekinesis boy stop up active volcano"
although you and i in the same headline for any reason felt just as sweet.

and we made a good team.
we worked well together.
swooping down from the heavens via our shared gift of flight
gliding actually
because when you find someone who fits you like that
like a good sneaker
or a warm blanket
you try to stay above the ground a little more often.
or as much as you can.

and it was certainly an asset to us, madame bat.

it's so much easier to date a girl who works the same hours.
it's nice to have a girlfriend who understands you.
and it got us membership into the justice collective
which is only like the x-men for los angeles super heroes.

thanks a million, madame,
for letting me patrol with captain fast and the green rhino on
wednesday nights.
thanks for rescuing me from the clutches of doctor nefarious
that one time.
okay, every time.
thanks for keeping an extra beer in the fridge for me.
you are the super glue that holds this relationship all the way tight.

we are mutants enamored
and our kids may be bigheaded leather-winged freaks
but they will be loved.
and that's what being a hero is all about.


## Batman's Attraction
Michael Brown

It was her everyday shape
that caught his eye:
thick waist, round shoulders,
circular breasts, straight hips,
and thighs like an Olympic skater.
They had their commonality in common.
No super powers. Super attitude
when they were costumed-the only
thing they needed to hide
when they were dressed for day work.
How else do we recognize those we love
except their likeness validates us
by a completeness that is ourselves?
Mundane days they dress as others do
and do the jobs the world offers.
When superior device and determination
are called forth by evil, they turn
from ordinary tasks as plainly
as ordinary folk, so when they come home,
they sleep together in peace.
He told her that.
For a moment, he almost doubted.
She almost smiled.
Both hesitated because they knew
when a hero falls, all is lost.


## Wonder Woman
Jamie Burgess

Let me be your make wonder woman
making you wonder like a mystery
reaching highs with wit and strategy
finding means to solve me.
Reveal me slowly like stages set dramatically,
uncovering my secret identity.
Unwrap me like a surprise at any given time
every single time collecting pieces of me
like clues to an irresistible puzzle
always challenging you.
Let me be your make wonder woman
because nothing is made like history
and possibility goes on infinitely.

Let me be your have wonder woman,
having you wonder like an idea
still painstakingly unclear
drawing answers through logic with care.
True heroes ignore boundaries and fear
allowing moments to skyrocket
like fireworks adventures appear
mortality loses inevitability
becoming one thought swirling
into a larger body of comprehensibility.
Let me be your have wonder woman
because having wonder surround the ordinary
stirs transformations evoking something extraordinary.

Let me be your create wonder woman
creating wonder like magic by believing it,
as super powers triumph the reality set
soaring in the good as the going gets.
Count on time to change everyday,
taking it formless for molding like clay
turning small celebrations into holidays.
Divine forces are by design
matching earth to heaven just like time
again and again.

Let me be your create wonder woman
because creating wonder makes sunsets spectacular
existing beauty to sharing beholders.
Realize love only wins by surrender.
Let me be your wonder woman
as I wonder all about you.


## Superman's Girl
Leigh Harrison

Sometimes I wanted to be Lois Lane.
Lois -- forever the spunky "good girl" --
perky, professional, well-organized.
Perpetually undaunted Daily Planet
gal reporter who always got her scoop.
Businesslike, I'd be dressed modestly,
that neat, demure, pageboy hairstyle
a blue-black raven's wing, eternally
on my pert, inquisitive head.  Wanted
to grow up like her -- career-minded,
perhaps a modest independent streak.

But mostly, I wanted to be Lana Lang,
because the bad girls had all the fun.
I imagined tossing my flaming red mane,
letting it flounce around my bare neck,
insinuating myself, my unruly curls, on
Superman's shoulder, pressing my breasts

against the S on his well-toned chest.
I'd put on bold, crimson lipstick, flirt
with all the guys in Clark's newsroom.
I'd wear my skirts hiked up to here,
casually sashay amid the noir streets,
stiletto heels clicking on cobblestones
while stray bullets zinged around me.
I'd be his naughty, willful, erotic muse,
pout until Superman bravely rescued me --
from time-traveling Terran mobsters,
or from Lex Luthor, or Bizzaro World,
from aliens abducting Earth women,
metallic-skinned robots from Xenon,
creatures with eerie death rays.

Later, when he'd pulled me tenderly
from the smoking wreckage of a train,
or the villains' underwater cave where I'd
been captive, I'd let him embrace me
in those magnificently-muscled arms,
bat my eyelashes, linger on that curl
that never quite deserted his forehead,
brazenly tongue-kiss him, over and over,
until he peeled off those smooth red boots
below his perfectly sculpted thighs,
his indestructible cape and costume
tumbling to the ground all around us.

## Gamma Male
Tod Caviness

Hulk is strongest one there is!
Hulk know this
because Hulk build prison
even Hulk cannot escape from.
Puny humans might say, "Love!
Love is Hulk's prison."
No.
Hulk know what metaphor is.
Metaphor is toy for puny humans
who get bored with dictionaries.
Hulk not blame you.
But Hulk know what love is too.
Love is Betty.
Hulk's prison is Hulk's prison.
Hulk take Betty on date last month.
Tenth anniversary.
Hulk pick Betty up at army base
and puny humans celebrate,
shoot fireworks into sky
as Hulk jump away
but Betty not feel magic.
Hulk not understand.
Hulk plant redwood flowers

in desert for Betty,
make cow for dinner,
Hulk wear tight pants for Betty!
But Betty only cry
and throw up.
Then Hulk understand.
Betty afraid.
Puny humans always come
and take Betty away
and Hulk not offer security
like Bill Cosby
so hulk get to work right away.
Hulk build dream house in desert:
Picket fence of old bazookas,
shingles of helicopter blades,
thickest walls of diamond bricks!
Hulk even lay kitchen tile.
And guess what Betty say?
Hulk hear Betty say,
"Bruce, where are you?"
Bruce.
Betty's ex-boyfriend.
Puniest of puny humans
with handshake like jellyfish
and voice of kitten in puberty.
Betty never cry in front of Bruce.
Betty cry alone.
Why Betty want something
Betty no can have?
Hulk put foot down.
"Betty sleep on couch," Hulk say.
In morning Hulk make omelet.
Maybe Betty apologize
for putting wall between Hulk.
Hulk smash emotional walls!
Prison walls,
not so much.
Hulk make dream house
too big, too strong.
Front door, too small.
For Hulk.
When Betty come back someday
house will be better.
Hulk will clean out cow bones
and figure out indoor plumbing.
In meantime, Hulk sleep
and Hulk dream sometimes.
In dream Hulk is pink
and small and alone.
Hulk make scratches on paper
Hulk no can understand.
Maybe cake recipe.
Maybe formula for science.
Maybe love letter
with stupid metaphor.

Behind Hulk there is sound
that echoes like Grand Canyon screams

and is either bombs
falling outside
or Betty knocking.
When Hulk is finished
Hulk will answer the door
and we will go
someplace green.


## Robin's Lament
Stacie Boschma

Alfred says "Come quick!
The Bat Signal is on, sir!"
as our bed grows cold.


## Doom Patrol Haiku
Ryk McIntyre

I'm not "Robot Man"-
I'm a brain in a robot
body. I miss beer


## Logan
David Keali'i

There's something that should be admitted.
Okay.
Something I want to admit.

When I was a teenager, one of my first erotic dreams
involved us kissing.
I know. Big shock.

You never seemed like my type: not even five and a half,
rough along the edges, and you wore way too much flannel.
Oh. And the hair.
Dear God that hair style should have
stayed in the wild or at least the 80's.

I still wonder why out of all the X-Men, you were the one.
I tend to think that it's your personality.
You were always good to Kitty and Jubilee,
you teased Slim, accepted Kurt like no one else did
and I found your heartache over Red sweet.

Of course you never could hide your respect for the Prof.
Never could escape that past.
Never could figure out women.

That dream was a "Snikt!" that shook me
from fantasy.
Besides, I always thought that despite
the rough exterior,
you would have made a great lover.

Just saying.


## In Black and White
Beverly Wilkinson

the first day we met at summer camp
she was alone in the lunch room
head propped on hand
pushing fingernail crescents
into the bread of her sandwich

I'm a sucker for freckles

sitting next to her
I made coy sideways glances
until she held out her hand
offering me the white and red striped candy
that will precede her name from this day forward

no one ever gave me credit for that one

it was then that I pledged my devotion to her
promised her an eternity of desires
there is love in everything I do

I call her "sir" as an inside joke
in the paper and pencil of our lives
I appear not to know any better
or have a misguided sense of manners
but when we are folded away
where no one can see us
when the blood quickens under our skin
and her breath fogs my glasses
she listens to me like I am the one
who drew our world

I forgive her for passing me off as a servant
for the eye rolls she thinks I never see
I forgive the oh-so-obvious use
of Chuck as a beard
I know, out of the whole gang, I'm the smart one
I am amused by the people
who refuse to see this for what it is
angered by the ones with awareness who judge

until you have lived every moment of your existence
within four bold and rigidly straight lines
you can't tell me anything

some people live their lies so hard
they wear the ligature marks
like a signature t-shirt
maybe the guy with the pencil is God
showing us that love can easily be found anywhere
on a weekday
in black or white
or in the blaringly beautiful color
of a Sunday morning
but you have to look closely
and you may even have to read
between the lines

## Headlines
Robert "Ducky" McAuslan

queer community doubts
superman's supposed straightness
breeders are troubled

batgirl comes out
who knew? gorgeous hair
world did not crumble

the hidden frontiers
homosexuals in space
like fags just got there

warning-man of steel
may steal your man or husband
kryptonite sales up!

lesbian batgirl
shaves head, buys tool belt, gets date
bush trembles, earth moves

space is a long bore
janeway, seven of nine
need i say any more

comics or star ships
everyday advocate heroes
queers are everywhere

for all the doubters
i present one example
charles and magneto

subtle line spoken
you know me too well xavier
makes my point proven

batman fans got scared
they thought i was going there
nah, they're just "friends"

you must realize though
robins not gay, batman is
robin's a house boy


## The Big Bad Queer Wolf Remembers High School
Amanda Kail

Dear Jack,

You always knew all the other boys
were in love with you, your
sculpted pale and perfect ribcage,
your cock-eyed passion.  Jealously, I

managed to seduce you just once, just
because I wanted to
split you open, find out why
you were always the protagonist.  You explained in the
dark of your mother's basement that
this is where you brought
young women, like you were some
sort of Victorian master
and I a hopeful girl from your
village.

Even now, I can't believe how easily
you accepted the disguise I pulled to get
you naked, my rows of aching teeth
hidden behind full, sticky lips.  You
kept saying, "I don't know what it is,
why you attract me now, at this moment."
I smiled, rolled warm and full in your arms,
a rigid wolfboy hiding in a woman's body.
By morning I was bleeding heavily into
your flannel sheets.  I pulled
the blankets just so, slid up
and into my dress and attempted to
feel used when you ignored me for
the rest of the day, at the coffee shop
where admiring boys spat like men,
talking whiskey and Greek classics.  But instead
I left

without saying goodbye, deeply satisfied by
the blood i discarded
in your bed.

# Night on Snake Mountain

(for Jon Wolf)
Morris Stegosaurus

Once

Skeletor and Charybdis shared a suite in a castle high atop Snake Mountain.

Each night, Charybdis would massage
Skeletor's hollow sockets with her tentacles
and he would moan so low as to make madmen tremble.
So tenderly they stroked and sighed,
so widely stretched their love
that even the angels forgot to dance
and stumbled like penguins drunk
on kahlua and cocoa.

But God is a Fuckerhead,
as sure as Monday tastes like onion
and the only King of Spain
has mustard in his eyes:

God likes a good joke.
Yeah. He likes to fuck around.

Witnessing the way Skeletor's burnished bones
slip between Charybdis' most nautical flesh
like a club-sandwich-hold-the-mayo,
God decides to test the mettle of their affection:

In His impossibly broad fists,
God grabs spears of asparagus by the thousand
and casts them upon the lovers with more force
than a bull battering a glass anvil

But Charybdis only swells wide
and swallows them up like
a thunderhead inhaling the moon
Next He grabs a panoply of Lego blocks:
There are Star Wars Legos and Pirate Legos
and Space Station Legos and Castle Legos
and Bionicle Legos, and yes, even He-Man Legos
and, oh, most terrible of terrors: even Duplos
those most destructive and massive of plastic building blocks,
deadly when flung with the laser-like precision of a wrathful deity--

But Skeletor barely looks up from snogging his amore
to bat the onslaught aside with his Havok Staff,
*bat*!*bat*!*bat*
smacking with characteristic aplomb.

Never one to be thwarted, Our Lord and Master
Snatches up all His old CDs:
His Counting Crows and His Cranberries,
His Sarah McLachlan and His Sheryl Crow,

Smashing Pumpkins and Soundgarden,
Red Hot Chili Peppers and Jamiroquai
and Toad the Wet Sprocket, as well.

He hones them all on a grindstone
crafted from the backs of titans
to a sharpness fine enough to slice
through the very concept of morality
and flings them, each in turn,
at the offending couple.
Skeletor tries to fend off the vile discs,
but his Havok Staff is cleft in twain
by the Foo Fighters.
Left undefended, Charybdis's loving tentacles
are severed in turn, by Gin Blossoms, REM and Cake.

A final Built to Spill splits Skeletor's skull from neck:
it rolls slowly across the cobblestone floor,
to come to rest against Charybdis's now limb-less frame.

Lame, but not yet defeated, Charybdis again stretches wide her maw
and engulfs the skull of her beloved.
Now sated, she growls, "Do your worst,
Oh most dastardly of deities,
You can throw all manner of vegetable,
Children's toy,
or musical reproduction
at us, but now we can never be separated,
my love shall live inside me forever"

From deep within her belly,
Skeletor cackles defiance.

His frustration welling within Him,
The Lord swells, then bursts like
a cherry bomb, spattering all Eternia
with His divine remains.

In time, Charybdis slides and slithers her way
back to her coastal abode,
returns to a life of slurping sailors
like so much grape soda,
but she knows:
her love will be with her, always:
cackling like a rat with a patch of
ham clutched between its paws.

## When My Great-Grandmother Carmilla Met Count Dracula
Stefan Sencerz

Slowly, Dark Lord enters her
den, right when she buried Uncle Ben.

My great-grandmother Duchess Carmilla
greets him with homemade brownies and pots
full of tea, speaks warmly, shifting her veil:
"So very nice to see you, Sir!"

"So nice to see you," he replies
enchanted by her lustrous eyes.

In front of a covered mirror she stands
in a dark widow's gown and a little black hat
but the way she smiles and holds her hands
clearly implies, "We are just friends."

"Shit!" He swears, for it is obvious
she will be careful and cautious
and he hates it, he wants her naked
he craves her body. To wit, he is a dog.

But she ain't easy-
she is my blood.

And so, he visits her each night,
plays game of chess, toys with her mind,
springs upon her the King's Gambit, attacks,
squeezes, almost bursts through her lines.

She defends very well, does not resign,
and at the end gives him headache.

"Por favor! Agarrame la cabeza!"
"Hold my head in your hands!" he begs.
She tries to help, removes his furs,
leans his huge sword against the wall,
loosens his tie, holds his head tight,
her hands are working up and down.

"I'll make this widow peak," he dreams
looking upon her pallid neck.

But she will not submit quite yet,
will not go down on her back.

Finally, long after midnight,
a cock crows and again and again

the time's ripe, she nips him deeply,
sucks, savors blood from his vein;
gives him the thrill of his life-
the bliss few mortals have survived.

Such a sweet boy he was,
so nicely he had smiled.
Sure, he had a little
vice here and there,
yet overall was so much fun.
But then he met Granny Carmilla,
and she has ruined the son of a gun.

# Details of the Endless
Aaron Enskat

The first thing that people noticed?
Nothing was quite right,
everything tasted like chicken.
Mirror images took on Monet tones,
lovers could no longer find those special spots,
air traffic controllers became slightly less suicidal,
and ivory towered academics revised
their opinions of performance poetry.
Yup, the world turned right wonky the day
Detail of the Endless took the night off.

Mental Health Break, she called it.
She had grown tired of being called nit-picky,
and insufferable; of having lovers leave
saying "the Devil's in the Details...". And he was,
even Lucifer called her controlling in bed.
And being left out of a certain
critically acclaimed account
of her unusual family by
Mr. "Only Likes Some Details" Gaiman
just because the number seven seems so much
more mystical than eight.   Fucking wanker.

So, she appeared in her twin brother's gallery
and said, "Destiny, I'm off like a bullet-point."
And he nodded (for it was written that he would),
shifted the weight of book,
continued along his garden maze.
That night, Dream walked his domain
as it deteriorated into rough estimates of emotion,
leaving people to wake from sleep
remembering nothing but disembodied passion,
intangible terror, or ethereal whimsy.
Stoically, Dream sat within his haze shrouded castle,
waiting for Detail of the Endless to return.

That night, Despair met Desire in a hurricane
that looked like angry mist trying to lose weight.
They held each other close, unsure
how their work could continue.
For what is desire but the hunger for detail?
what is Despair, but the fear of it?
That night, Destruction painted and composed,
sculpted and danced and laughed to himself,
realizing that lack of detail improved his art
immensely.  Delirium shaved opalescent fish.

The night Detail took herself a little break,
she met her younger sister, Death.
They played Skeeball and Galaga in an
old bowling alley in Peoria, and she asked

"Death, in the end, what does it all matter?"
Death smiled, handed her a hot dog and a wooden ball,
both so rich in their simple shapes.
"Let's keep playing," she said,
"your turn is almost up."


## Thor
David Surrette

He never looked right at you.
He tilted his head, blond hair to his shoulders,
squinted even at midnight
to limit what he took in.
I only knew Him in summer

where a belt, gloves, and a hammer are hard to hide,
but He possessed them I am sure.
On Thursday evenings,
He fought giants one at a time.
He would tilt his head, squint,

and the guy would shrink before our eyes
and before he could grow back,
he was on the ground, calling for his uncle.
He confused us for a while with a dark-haired girl
whom He couldn't keep happy.

Long blonde hair like summer corn came later.
She combed it gold just for Him
He came to visit me as I lay almost dying,
but even He couldn't get past the night nurse.
I watched Monterey Pop in a morphine haze:

Joplin made me eat her sins.
She made me drink her sorrows.
He would do the same.
Like Woodstock, everyone claimed
they were there, but I'll forever believe

he died alone.


## Nightcrawler
James "J*me" Caroline

A rabble of anger circled my Mother,
waving torches at the bundle in her arms-
devil's tail wagged out behind baby features.
She fled the villagers childless;
left me on a sprig of Jasmine
blue as a shadow's rim,
eyes the color of angels fear.

I grew up in the circus
among gypsy fortune tellers
and knife throwers,
tramps, thieves, white shirt brawlers.
I dove from the top of the reddest tent
spiraling through cables
a body of springs and banding
like untwisting a garland of thorns
above spectators heads.
I flew

wire to wire hand over foot
a winged bullet
too stupid to know
I'd been kicked into motion
by the black boot of God.

Teleporting is
like unzipping the air.

My stepbrother was a dancer-
bent knee and kick
smile spinning on one leg.
Stefan the gypsy Prince
terrified of the madness
and magic he might carry in his blood.

To leave you
I tear open reality and leap.
There are tiny moments
where the earth spins without me.
I travel hell;
am followed out
by unfurling brimstone
and sulfur.

He was gold and jewel-
his mother's hearth.
He left the wagon,
became a child killer,
preyed on the softest grace in babies.
He said it was like
growing more mouths on his body-
a 2nd thirsty heart
that it could not be helped.
There was a struggle
something near stumbling while marching,
realizing he was dead
when I felt the bones in his neck
shuffling like marbles beneath his skin.
That is when I began praying

***

I reappear whole
grinning

fanged and playful
a monster conceding love

when I started to make the sign of the cross-
head, heart, each arm
when holy became weight
a pulsing ruby as my axis.

chased by memory
by what I left in the light

## Protective Clothing Siesta
Tom Daley

If you conjure him, he will come to light.
Elastic as a ghost,
he flickers the warehouse corridor
with encroaching fire.

Under his lab coat,
reds and blacks lit at his pubic arch
checkerboard their way up
the wishbones of your nerves.

He threads through the rubber bales,
a still water born
of lips canned in their own juice.

His shape frescoes the hall wall
in mechanical shadows, his watch alarmed
for an afternoon nap in the nurse's office
where you both woke up
clammy on the examining table.

He is cold as a filament
after Oklahoma ice storms.
Over his pointed ears, wooly hairlets
prickle and baa.

After the siesta, he daubed
petroleum jelly pictograms on the nurse's door.
You traded latex for triage.

Locksmith of oblivion, he
has tangled you in translucence.  Now you are
a keyhole through which
nothing more perilous than sleep
can ever shine.

# I Rule, Therefore I Am
The Klute

I never wanted to be a superior.
On the playground,
When the other boys were scaling the jungle gym as Spiderman,
Or running around with a makeshift cape
Fashioned from a plastic lunchroom tablecloth,
I would be alone in the sandbox,
Plotting.

I never wanted to be superior.
Even as a little kid I never saw the allure.
It was all work and no play.
Danger was around every corner
And I wanted to be able to go places without being set upon
By an army of laser-wielding spider robots.
I mean, how do they sell people on this Superman trip?

"So, let me get this straight,
I get to risk my life- for free- saving the world from certain death,
And then I get to go work at a dead-end desk job
Where my insurance plan doesn't cover treatment
for poison gas exposure or death ray burns?
Awesome! Where do I sign up!?!?"

No thank you.
The flip side however, Super Villainy, is a pretty sweet gig.
You get neat gadgets, like atomic psychofrakulaters,
Or the aforementioned laser-wielding spider robots.
Instead of a lame catch phrase like "Shazam!" or "Up, Up, and Away!"
You get an evil laugh that's accentuated
with big, bold capital letters that always go off panel!
Your costume isn't some homo-erotic pastel one-piece.
It's probably black with a majestic sweep,
Or a classic suit with a nice trim.
As a super villain, you get henchmen with metal teeth
Instead of sidekicks with abandonment issues.
Your girlfriend isn't the prim-and-proper Lois Lane or Mary-Jane
Who'll only put out when you're in costume.
As a super villain, you'll get women who appreciate the sensitive soul
Behind the metal mask and 40-foot high video monitors,
And for whom foreplay is my monologue
About how one day I will rule the world with an iron fist.

You've got focus-
You're not trying to discover the truth behind your mysterious origins
While bringing your parent's killers to justice,
And trying to fit in to a world that would shun you
if they only knew your terrible secret.
No, for you it's:
Step One: Take over the world
Step Two: Enjoy!

Best of all, you're not bound by the rules-
but the other guy is.

Captain Sunshine can't send Wonder Boy off to die to cover his escape-
But I can.
In fact all of you are just pawns in my plans for world domination,
And if I have to sacrifice you to see those plans come to fruition?
Well, that's just one less mouth to feed in the new world order.

And I'm cool with that, because I'm a super villain.
I always wanted to be a super villain.
I would laugh when the Spiderman wannabe fell
from the jungle gym to the concrete jungle below,
Or when little Jimmy's plastic lunchroom cape would snag on a door
And drop him like Kryptonite.

But I wouldn't laugh because I was evil,
(well, maybe a tad);
I just knew, from the security of my sandbox sanctum, that
they were suffering the inevitable fate of every superior
They were chumps.
Suckers.
Fools.
And I'll show them!
I'll show them all!


## Spherical Man
Mike McGee

Wherever there is suffering
and microwaveable food
I'll be there
Wherever there is injustice
and nachos
I'll be there
Wherever there is crime
near an open deli

I'll be there
In a world where scrawny super-heroes will eventually fail
The people need a man of substance
A man of true girth
Someone who can save the world...before dinner time
That man is me

and I...
...I am Spherical Man
S is for Super
As in supermarket
As in let's go to the supermarket and buy some food
That would be Super!
P is for Posse
As in I am my own posse
H is for Hungry
As in all the time
As in, "Are you gonna finish that?"
E is for Enormous
Every where you look, there I am

R is for Rolls
I mean, who doesn't like hot, buttery rolls?
I is for Intelligence
You have to be smart to know how to keep the weight on
To know which foods are good for you
and which foods are good to you
C is for Cunning
Like rewrapping Twinkies as energy bars
A is for Attitude
Damn right I want it super-sized, bitch!
L is for Lurid
I mean, anybody whose clothing size
begins with Triple-X
must be good with their mouth!

S-P-H-E-R-I-C-A-L

Look, up in the sky, it's a moose
No, it's a beach ball
No, it's a couch
NO! I'm Spherical Man!
I can leap a buffet table with a running start!
My cannonball is revered at every public swimming pool!
I faster than your average three-legged dog on heroin!
By day
I'm a mild-mannered Video Game Tester
By night
I'm still a mild-mannered Video Game Tester
only I wear an intimidating cape and really aggressive tights.

Join forces with me now
Let us rid the world of Jenny Craig and her satanic cult
We must stop Richard Simmons before he has the whole world
greased up and wearing short-shorts
Come together with me and my sidekick Feedbag!
We will move toward a world with more cushion for the pushin'!
A community where we embrace those bigger than us
knowing we may never touch fingers
A universe where breakfast is an excuse to miss work

Superman has Kryptonite
I have Slim Fast
But my bladder can hold far more than his!
And I am three-dimensional, therefore
I am Spherical Man!


## Hey Skinny!
Christian Drake

Yer ribs are showing!

And if you've ever read comic books, you know what happens next.
Beach Bully stiff-arms Beanpole in the face,

Brunette Bimbo mocks him.
Beanpole goes home, gives an effeminate little kick,
orders the free Charles Atlas Dynamic Tension booklet,
and fifteen minutes later, he's jacked like a war machine,
and strangely enough, looks exactly identical to the Beach Bully
except for different-colored swimming trunks.
Former Beanpole goes back to the beach,
sucker-punches Bully in the throat. Bully looks surprised,
because Beanpole gained 100 pounds of muscle,
a wider jaw and a better hairdo inside of one afternoon.
Brunette Bimbo swoons, "What A Man!"
And I, at seventeen, five-foot-ten and 125 pounds,
wanted to be an Atlas Man. With every issue of the Incredible Hulk,
I contemplated whether to order the free booklet so I could get girls
or the x-ray glasses that just let me see through girls' clothing,
while, curiously, allowing me to see my own skeleton.
But you could already see my skeleton.
It's not that my metabolism was high, it's that I was eating for two:
me and the small wolverine in my thoracic cavity.
And I'm not asking you to pity me because I'm skinny;
I'm asking you to fear me because I'm skinny.
Because skinny boys are angry little weasels.
Football players use us as Q-tips.
We dodge military men like tanks in Tiananmen Square.
We never beat our dads at arm-wrestling.
I may be skinny, but my rage is Gilbert Grape's mom.
And if you ever read comic books, you know that the Incredible Hulk
was the football player inside every science geek.
And Captain America was once a skinny blond kid, too,
until the government "super serum"
made his chest wide enough to wear the flag.
Because Captain America is like our country:
picked on when it was young, it juiced itself up
until it looked just like the bully.
And that's all men really want: to beat our bullies.
We're pumping iron and shooting our "super serum."
Gonna beat the home run record, gonna be Governor of California.
Gonna beat up our step dads someday.
And I remember my beach bully, the Christian kid at summer camp.
I used to quote the bible at him while he beat me up.
I remember the day I discovered that when I got him in the water,
the buoyancy made featherweights of both of us.
I was a ten-year old alligator wrestler,
shoving his head underwater like a witch,
smashing him over and over with a tennis ball fist
clenched so tight it was a rock.
And when the lifeguard pried us apart, bloody-nosed,
I wept so hard my wishbone ribs threatened to break,
because I finally knew what it was to be a man,
an Atlas Man, because now I felt the weight
of the world on my tiny shoulders.

# Gadarene
Jack McCarthy

I'm the new face on
the bridge of the Enterprise
with Kirk and Spock and Bones
as Scotty's voice intones over the intercom
"I'm givin' ye all she's got, Captain--"
and Sulu and Uhuru and me,
Ensign O'Malley- Ensign O'Malley?
Dead meat, Ensign O'Malley.
I never make it past the first scene.
I live only in reruns.
You can see me also on Rocky and Bullwinkle,
the ticker tape parade that celebrates
Mr. Peabody and Sherman.
I'm the little guy with the broom
sweeping up the ticker tape.
I'm the poet whose submissions come back
not just unpublished, but unopened
because I have this Twilight Zone knack
of submitting to magazines
that are about to fold up shop.
I'm the unknown soldier,
the player to be named later,
the child on the milk carton-
no, I'm the adult with whom that child
was last seen. The guy who knocked
on the door of the shelter five minutes
after it was locked up tight for the night.
I called the suicide hotline and they put me
on hold, I'm everyone who ever fell
through a hole in a safety net.
I'm the working stiff whose only investment
ever was my years of coming home late
to cold suppers long after my kids were
in bed. Tonight's lead story is your stock
went up when I got downsized.
I'm the disgruntled
former employee
that you'll never recognize
until I'm squinting at you
over the dark eye of an Uzi.
I am the silent Indian
who haunts the second darkest recess
of the American conscience-
even I don't go into the corner
where the slaves are kept.
I am the Gadarene,
called into existence for the sole purpose
of being possessed by your demons
and carrying them over a cliff
with me.
You have a life only because
you've been assigned one

as part of this experiment-
I'm in the control group;
me they gave a placebo.
I'm not a human being,
I just play one on the street.
I'm none of the above.
I raised my hand
only to claim my seat
but now that I have your attention,
I find that I do have one thing to say:
I'm going to keep coming.
You can't make me
go away.


## "Take Him Back, Mei Ling"
Ry Eff

I have to get this off my chest.
I am lost in
Jonah Hex's labyrinth,
wringing hands hard enough
to raise the smell of
sulfur while he picks
off bad guys with
a dose of Southern
give-it-to-'em-good.

What first struck me (beautiful)
about Jonah was that tomahawk scar
on his face:
high proof of red light murder,
that mean mother.
Of slow lonesome battles
in the swamps.  Being born in
shallow end New England,
my feet are dry
deep in the Mason-Dixon.

Oh, the shame of rooting for a
Confederate diehard and not
knowing how to stop!

It's true:
I'm invisible enough already,
uncomfortable when on fire,
and I'm positive the
Mr. Fantastic complex
would wrap me with skin,
choked like snake food
in my own arms.

It's true, his wife left him.

It's true, he assassinated Superman.
Still, every inch of his action
strikes a match or two
for good taste. . .
(Ahem)...to mask that awful stink.

Jonah lost me along the way
as he woke up in the future,
hard-grin trailblazer
stacked illogically next to
skyscrapers and billboards,
chaw drip stuck to his bottom lip.

Hex caught in a small city world
and bored to wit's end as
I'm living near hardwood gallows
comfortable with murder,
writing wrongs along the way.

Men made of ink don't have chests
burdened with circumstance,
though we do. Inkmen pull
the trigger twice.

Fleshmen have the shotgun road behind,
but we shake off the dust.

I have empty pens for six-shooters,
but the whiskey still tastes the same.


## The Cajun X-Man
Steve Subrizi

So much depends
upon
Gambit kicking your
ass
With his Adamantium
staff
and kinetically charged
cards.


## The Four Seasons of Super Heroes
Len Germinara

1.

In summer I read Marvel comics
Flash light and worn blanket
The stars of Alpha Centauri
My neon soliloquy

I want to be Captain America
Pathos the driving force in my fantasy life
Made real in holding that course
Paper with the glossy wrapper
Opposed to reality

I needed someone to spell the sound of a nose breaking
Thank you Stan Lee

2.

Fall, I visit Valhalla
The gravitational pull inexorable
Thor's THHHWOKK blocked out
In an arch from hip
To point of impact

Most amazed I ever made it this far
I only wanted a shield to ward off bullets
Something to hide behind
While I fired crabapple invectives
At passerbys

3.

In winter I met Wonder Woman
On her way to work
All clogs and apple cheeked
Speculative fiction in her wake
Now I ride the passenger seat
In the invisible jet
I drive a car with a blue "On-Star" button
Carry in the palm of my hand all I need
I beam
I live long
I prosper
Zoom, Zoom…
Zoom

4.

In just spring
I walk the Salt marsh
She guards
Ancient spoken word
Ankle deep in ooze
Turning over rocks
Looking for new language
Delve the acronym
Pulling the plum
in poetry's soul
Spring is like a perhaps hand
Mechanically enhanced.

# Mandrake the Magician
Patricia Cosentino

Mandrake The Magician,
he was my man.
Hero of the "Super vs Villain".

1920's serials were black and white,
but that's how Mandrake saw The Truth:
always as fine a line as mustache over
strong jaw. Even Umberto Eco
admired him, transforming
this fearless wizard into Italian.

When I was a kid- and it was Saturday mornings-
we had Nana's parlor all to ourselves.
We'd play: "Stars Of The Funnies"
(this was the 1930's, you understand)
Bob would be Mandrake The Magician, I had to be The Wasp,
Phyllis, who was younger, was always the "Glamorous Lady In Distress";
our old player-piano was the futuristic "Computer!"
With crystal earphones we'd "transmit codes"
by sticking wire-ends into piano parts.

Of course, The Wasp was never a match
for Mandrake and Lothar, the Ebony Prince Of Destiny!
We took turns with the roles we played,
but Good conquered Evil, always.
Manadrake's "Abra-Cadabra!" sanctioned
the Pathway to Righteousness.


# Star Wars Limericks
Andrew Watt

A pretty sweet princess named Leia,
thought Solo too much of a playa,
so she kissed with her tongue,
Luke Skywalker young,
which was so wrong, on more than one laya.

A hunter of bounties named Fett
captured Han Solo for debt.
To keep him held tight,
Fett used carbonite,
in a clear case of freeze and forget.

The council of Jedis sent just two
to deal with the strife on Naboo,
secure in the notion
the Trade Federation
would still have no clue what to do.

The Pacifist Queen of Naboo
first ran the blockade, and got through.
Her passion and need
saved the people of Theed,
while Palpatine's power just grew.

Those clever accountants and clerks
weren't your average jerks:
Though one Death Star would do,
they bought and built two.
and charged both to an Empire's perks.

First burned up, then sealed in black leather,
Darth Vader felt under the weather:
"Though Paul Stanley of KISS
might find this get-up pure bliss,
there are itches you can't reach with a feather."

The Millennium Falcon, it's true,
cannot be regarded as new;
Still, she's famed for her speed
and can vanish at need
from an Imperial frigate or two.

## Purple
Trevor Byrne-Smith

In Gotham City, keeping law and order is not unlike
playing Jenga with speed freaks.
This city has a precarious pH tonight,
tipping a little towards acid.  Batman's seen worse.

The streets are lined with infants under silent lullabies,
while jack-in-the-box serial men live beneath street lamps.
The Dark Knight remains perched at yellow alert.
That's when he hears it, like a rude interruption.
Flash of fire and the air cracks like a broken back,
fire devours the skyscraper like a predator,
The Bat-Signal seems superfluous now.

Batman, in four-point-stance, shifts weight to legs,
readies muscles and joints for battle but, before
feet part with rooftop, he smells that familiar
scratch-and-sniff scent, sees the brief flash of purple.
Smacking his bat gloves against his bat cowl he mutters:
"...Spoiler..."

Teenage girls from the suburbs should not fight crime.
Stephanie Brown was born to be the next Jason Todd.
Daughter of a question mark copycat thief,
Stephanie grew up in the crack between bed and wall,
dreaming of rooftop acrobatics, she fell in love with the night.

Conquering rooftops,
Spoiler became the guardian of suburbia,
She was never very good at what she did.
Born under an eclipse of sin, she envied uncarved marble
and fought every day to unmake the statue
she was made into before birth.

She was always the unwanted child of the Bat-Family.
When she graduated herself into Gotham,
she was treated as a liability.  Her boyfriend, Robin,
loved her like Tupperware loves week-old meat

She battled back every demon this city could spit up
with frantic baby fists until, slick with blood,
her hands could no longer carry her up Gotham's towers.
She was never very good at what she did.
She was born to be the next Jason Todd.

He was called Black Mask,
an unpoetic name for an unpoetic man
Whose single bullet- the clumsiest of all thieves-
robbed her of adulthood.  Beneath white sheets,

like an Angel. The red sound of heart monitors gave
the only announcement of life leaving body.
But defeat came long before death,
and Stephanie still fought and died a braver hero
than Kal-El will ever be.

She was forever overshadowed and untalented.  But hard work means nothing
when The Batman tattoos the words "Fuck Up!" on your forehead.
Now Spoiler's a footnote trying desperately to cling
to the bottom of the slippery pages of Gotham history.

But some nights,
when the cult of the Bat is short on soldiers,
rescued citizens report a flash of purple,
the scent of scratch-and-sniff perfume,
and a voice like a shouted whisper saying:

"Remember me.
I am a hero."


## Why Bruce's Gimmick Doesn't Fly in German
Robert S. Dunn

Ask yourself,
In all honesty —
If you were an
Escaped felon
In a graphic novel,
Would you really be
Intimidated
By a super hero named
"Die Fledermausench?"

# The Super Heroes' Ball
Rich Boucher

Captain America raises his glass,
and takes a sip of his vodka and tonic,
shooting a sly, sidelong
glance across the dance floor at Catwoman,
who isn't looking his way; she's bending down
to lace her boots.

"Holy Shit!", shouts Robin,
three sheets to the wind already,
drunk on Bud Light and teenage freedom,
(it is after eleven after all)
and he's raving on and on about how hot
all the super heroines are in here tonight.
Batman looks about ready to smack him one.

Every so often, amid the sea of voices
in every room in this grand place,
another is heard to say, "The Flash?
He was just here a minute ago.
No, I don't know where he is - oh, there he is!"

In the kitchen, coffee's perking in the back,
there are cooks shouting orders back and forth,
there's a mortar and pestle with rosemary and thyme,
there's wine being poured into fine crystal glasses,
there's Superman and Spiderman arguing passionately
about the U.S. in Iraq.

Thor is already bored and wanting
to take his entourage of supermodels someplace else.
Meanwhile, almost a quarter of a mile away,
two uniformed doormen at the gates to the estate
are trying in vain to explain
to Mr. Puff Q. Daddy, Esq.,
the difference between "ubiquity" and "superhuman."

There is a line fifteen heroes long waiting for the Hulk to get out of the bathroom.
I'd like to have been invited to this little soirée,
with all the lights and the music and the games and the gossip,
but I'm real- therefore I can't come.
Out on the balcony that overlooks
the mansion's sprawling drive,
it's a starry October night, clear
and with a chill in the air,
and out of earshot of the rest
Wonder Woman is making a clever pass at
Batgirl, who laughs,
blushing brightly at the Amazon's dirty joke.

Down below, in the orange and blue
of the moonlight and Japanese lanterns,
Aquaman leans up against the back of his Oldsmobile,
and weeps.

# Ballad of the Aqua Pussy
Robbie Q. Telfer

Aquaman was sick of being a pussy

He knew the Super Friends all dissed him behind his back
He knew they kept him around for laughs
He knew that despite whatever Wonder Women said
        She wasn't going to call him
He knew all of these things
His power:
The communication and control of anything that lived in water
Clearly, he was a pussy and he was seasick of it
After the Flash taped a "Grill Me" sign to his back
After Green Lantern froze his underwear for the 7th time
After he slipped on the cafeteria floor in his pool shoes and Superman and Batman high-
fived each other saying, "Huh huh, yeah!"
The only thing he knew, was that he was a super NERD

Freedom and justice and the American Way are fucking boring
when no one gives two ships about the water
After years of showing up with a crab army too late to help anyone out
It slowly began to sink in that his marine team had no business doing good
Aquaman, like Richard the III if he also were a pussy, decided to become a villain
None of those asshole Super Friends would suspect anything
And that's why it would be easy to get them out of the way

Luckily most kryptonite meteors go to the bottom of the ocean with
        -Satellites,
        -Ghost Ships,
        -Other plot devices,
And are collected by octopuses
Who then form basic chemical bonds with the kryptonite
And turn into what Aquaman dubbed either
"Death-o-puses" or "Octo-murderers."
Along with his other aqua-traps
He would go into the Halls of Justice the next day
And initiate the beginning of the end

He showed up a little later than his usually unnoticed punctuality,
Saw the Wonder Twins on the way and told them to leave,
That shit was going down,
And since they'd always been nice to him,
And his beef was with those super-jocks,
That they should just take their purple monkey
And get the fuck out.
With an aquatic arsenal packed in duffels
He marched into the Halls of Justice that day
And forever turned his back on
America
Love
And being a pussy

The carnage was surprisingly quick

A lawn-dart narwhal shot through Batman's heart,

Robin's own heart failing as a result
The Flash wasn't so fast underwater
        As the barracuda swarmed
And Green Lantern was utterly defenseless
        Because he could never believe his eyes
Superman's demise was delicious therapy
The octo-murders crawling all over his body
As he did a terrible death Rumba
To the tune of Aquaman's laughter

A tying up of Wonder Woman in her own Lasso of Truth
Revealed what Aquaman suspected but didn't want to hear
        -Yes, he was a pussy
        -No, no one respected him
        -Yes, she never even considered calling him
        -No, she didn't want to die

But now the Machiavelli-anchovy would forever be feared,
And he didn't care if everyone hated him.
If they wanted revenge for innocent's demise
They'd have to go under the waves
And talk to him.


## The Legion of Substitute Heroes
Chris O'Carroll

In pulp-and-bright-ink secret truth
I knew how strong and high I stood,
More than just sneakers and a bike
Familiar in the neighborhood.

Any day now natural law
Would open a loophole for me --
Some accident with gamma rays
Or lightning bolts or chemistry,

Some visitors from outer space
Scouting for virtue to reward
With powers that would render me
Uniquely mighty and adored.

*Legion of Super Heroes* mags
Portrayed the new life I would lead,
But introduced five other youths
Of whom it vexed my heart to read.

They sported special powers, too,
But theirs were kind of second-rate.
Substitute Heroes they were called.
I laughed, but mourned such pranks of fate.

Polar Boy, Fire Lad -- they fought crime
By wielding blasts of cold and flames.
I didn't need to tell you that;
You could have guessed it from their names.

Night Girl's super powers functioned
Only when she was in the dark.
(And every guy she dated tried
The same dumb "Kill the lights!" remark.)

Chlorophyll Kid made plants grow fast.
Stone Boy could turn his mortal clay
Into stone (duh).  What fun if he
And Matter Eater Lad were gay.

All wanted to be Legionnaires,
But theirs was not quite the right stuff.
Too poignant for mere mortal me
To see these kids not good enough.

Oh Lord, my yearning heart Thou knowest;
Tell me, I beseech Thee, am I
Destined for full-measure greatness,
Or earmarked for merely semi?


## Where Have They Gone?
Mareh Labenski

I've been looking up to the rooftops
Measuring their distance from
One to another by single bounds
And up to the skies
Trying for just a glimpse of a
Red cape
Or the shadow of an
Invisible lasso
Some signal in the sky shining
Against the dark night

But lately there haven't been any signs
No one climbing the
Sides of buildings
No masked man in the streets
Fighting for Justice with a vengeance
Where have all the super heroes gone?
The ones who continuously saved the world
Every Sunday morning on TV
And rescued women and orphans
In the pages I read with a flashlight
Under the blankets in bed
Long after lights out

As a small child I wanted to be them
Running around through the supermarket isles
My nylon cape fluttering behind me
With my underwear proudly worn
On the outside of my one piece pajamas with the feet
My mother cursing herself
For letting me get too far from the carriage

As she decided against having spinach as that night's vegetable
And made a mental note to check for
Radioactive spiders in the corners of my room
Where the wall met the ceiling

As I got older though I saw them
Less and less
My mother told me I couldn't
Take them to school with me anymore
And I could never find them in the pages of
My class textbooks or homework
And I think that's when they started
Not coming around so much anymore

So where have all the super heroes gone?
I thought I saw superman
On the street the other day
We go way back, you see
Back to the days when we used to
Snicker at the lunch table
And throw gum in Wonder Woman's hair
She was flat chested back then
But no one ever knew it because of the wonder bra
Until she showed me one day
In the locker room after gym class
Anyway I thought I saw him on the street
And I almost said to him
"See? I told you she swung both ways"
But he didn't stop to say hello
Or even make eye contact
So it couldn't have been him
Probably just someone that looked like him
With the same glasses and the suit
Maybe they had the same opthamologist
So where did all the super heroes go?

I still try to keep in touch with them
Every now and then sneaking peeks at the pages
At the comic shop in Washington Heights
Sometimes back at the one in Delran
But they never call, never write
Wolverine did drop me a line just the other day though
And we made a date to hit the movies
When he comes back to town sometime this may
Maybe then I'll try to rekindle my
Old friendship with Phoenix
And word will spread around

And Bruce and I will go for a joyride
Leaving Robin behind
And we'll hook up in the back of the Batmobile like old times
Making love with some pencils and a sketch pad
Or maybe I'll hook Aqua Man up with one of my girlfriends
She always said she liked to swim
And when the hype gets big enough

The super heroes will return
And it'll be just like they never left


## The Conflagration of '38
Matt Hopewell

June 1st, 1938:

The birth of a hero,
along with a new era-
not only of caped and masked men and women,
and villains bent on world domination-
but of a whole new universe with the boundaries
only of how far one can push one's imagination.
I speak, of course,
of Action Comics #1.

The first appearance of a hero, the first
hero to truly be considered "Super,"
A Kryptonian conceived in 1934,
considered "unbelievable" by publishers
until the summer of '38.
Which raises the question:
How dare they?
How dare they declare a creative concept
"too unbelievable" to be marketable?

I guess I can take solace in the fact that they were wrong.

Once the young minds of the era's imaginations were stimulated,
a floodgate was opened:
worlds were born in cartoonists' brains.  Outlandish universes
populated by heroes, anti-heroes, villains, aliens, monsters and robots.
Those of you who would argue that Batman was much cooler must consider:
Batman was created as a response to the popularity of Metropolis' titan!
This superist-of-heroes was a prototype, paving the way
for our Batmans, our Wonder Women, our Spidermen,
so a fair comparison can hardly be made.

All this is not to say that Action Comics #1 was the start of it all.

Nathaniel Hawthorn's "The Grey Champion" was published in 1885.
Other heroes like the Scarlet Pimpernel, Obadiah Oldbuck, Tarzan,
and Buck Rogers were all there before the Man of Steel.
But they served only as the kindling for the conflagration of '38.
No wild-man of the jungle could spark our imaginations like Clark,
no space-exploring sci-fi pulp could match the power
of our extraterrestrial juggernaut.

Because Siegel and Shuster asked us to suspend our disbelief:
to give our poetic faith to a world where evil has a face,
and good is clearly defined in terms that can only be considered "Super."
Imagine a universe where anything is possible, where worldwide
disaster is averted, miraculously, almost daily.

To believe, to have faith, that there are supernatural forces fighting
for good, and that good always prevails.

"Great Caesar's ghost," we need a man like that!
We need a world where things are easily defined,
if only to escape the terrors of reality long enough
to finish a comic book. Because it's a scary world,
and things are not always as they seem.
So don't be surprised
        If you see my eyes
                glancing to the sky
                        with the hopes
                        of seeing a blue-red bullet.

Because
If we believe strongly enough,
maybe, just maybe
some super hero might come
and save us all.


# Criticism Part I (with Great Power)
Curtis Meyer

      I was sitting in the break room with some time to kill before checking out, and
Mike and I were browsing through his newest shipment of comics. I was just commenting
how great an artist Adam Kubert is, when all of a sudden-
      "Ow can you read dose filtee tings?"
      It was Annette, a fellow employee, some 40 or 50 years old, and a former
resident of Jamaica. Now I digress, realizing I was 20-years old at the time, but I replied
with: "Comic books are fundamental in teaching kids appreciation of art, writing, and story
telling, while subconsciously enhancing the content of their vocabulary and sense of
imagination."
      Mike nodded, "'s true."
      Apparently my words sped over Annette's head faster than a speeding bullet:
"Dose tings are vile and nasty."
      Now, Annette is a conservative black woman who voted for Bush in the last
election solely because she agreed on his stances against abortion and gay marriage.
I could've told her how these issues had nothing to do with the economy, healthcare,
or any number of issues affecting her personal descent into poverty. But I don't make
personal attacks. I merely quipped, "At least I'm reading."
      "I'd radder not be able to read den read dose nasty tings."
      And the conversation pretty much ended there, with me turning my nose back
into the pages disgusted. It's been a defining incident for me. As I realized later on, as I
always do, I had said the wrong thing. I should have said, "If you can't read comic books,
you can't read the Bible either." But I don't blame Annette for being as close-minded as
she is. How would she know anything about how the concept of super-heroes is as old
as time itself, ranging from Gilgamesh, to Beowulf, to Hercules, Achilles, Perseus, and
Paris, to Samson, David, Moses, and Jesus himself? How would she understand the
ideal of a protecting figure more than human, and still ultimately capable of being undone
by a simple flaw like a mule's jaw, a weak heel, or Kryptonite? How would she know that
comic books continue the long line of verbal storytelling and moralistic implications set
forth in Aesop's fables, the Briar Rabbit parables told to the children of slaves, and the
toasts shared with ghetto youths, warning them away from drugs and a life of crime?

Annette may never know that the giant, mutant-hunting Sentinel robots in X-Men comics are an allusion to the Gestapo or that the Legacy Virus, which first infected mutants and spread to humans, is a metaphor for AIDS. Or sympathize with Nightcrawler, a character who's a priest in the body of a shunned demon. She many never understand that prejudice and heartache are completely relatable feelings, whether you're black, white, Jewish, homosexual, or even a comic book reader

But as my best friend tells me his parents found out that he's gay, my mind sinks back to the scene in X-Men 2, where Iceman's mother asks him, "Bobby, have you ever tried not being a mutant?" And it makes me think what I'd say if my kid came out of the closet-

"Dad? This is really hard for me, but I've decided I'm going to go crazy if I keep it in: Dad? I'm a mutant."

"Look my child, I love you no more or less for what you are. I have loved you since before you were born, and I will continue to love you still. I refuse to let you hide who you are and be ashamed. Your abilities were given to you with intent that you would one day know what to do with them, and I don't ever want you to view them as a stigma. Anything you can do should be seen as no less than a gift that proclaims your individuality. Don't ever let anyone tell you you are anything less than beautiful.

Just remember though, with great power comes great responsibility."

## The Miscegenator
Laura Swearingen-Steadwell

After millennia of war, God looked down from Heaven in great sadness.
Man, his favorite creation, was making a real asshole of himself:
whole factions of humans bent on killing one another off,
wave crashing into wave, tribe against tribe
as though difference were all that mattered.

God called in the heavenly consulate and took suggestions.
The counsel brainstormed, scribbling notes onto scrims of cloud in dewy ink
until it rained a host of peaceful ideas onto the city of Washington.
Finally, they found the answer,
the way to quell the mortals' bloodlust once and for all.
A force of such unbridled love,
it would overcome the hatred and xenophobia
that had plagued the people all existence.
The answer was me.

I am The Miscegenator, the destroyer of all things pure.
When I sneeze, neo-nazis whimper in their steel-toed boots,
the DAR run screaming from Constitution Hall!
Poor little KKK quiver in their hoods;
forlorn eugenicists weep in their rooms at night,
for I was sent to seduce every purebreed I can lay my thighs on,
every peach-skinned, gold-haired, blue-eyed virgin I can find.

I am the womb in which all become as one,
the womb that will spill out a million mixed-race babies-
and when they are born, I will name all the girls Grand Wizard,
and all the boys Louis, after Farrakhan.
I am the bless'd blender, She Who Mixeth, and all races tumble before my might!

You think you are safe in your hacienda, in your kibbutz?
No! Dojo and longhouse alike will fall!
You think your suburbs are safe? From me??
It is written: I am the undoing of every sect,
the unraveller of every genetic knot,
the one your teenaged children will take home and screw
regardless of your threats and pleas
and I will taint your bloodline, oh yes.

I am Sally Hemings.
Pocahontas.
Jack Johnson.
Desi Arnaz.
I am Yoko Ono, and it's time to break up the fucking band!

So to everyone who's with me:
everyone who's cursed with a limited gene pool-
islanders, rednecks, royalty, this means you-
to everyone who believes the world can change-
there is only one way out of this mess,
and it's right here.

God ordained me with the Womb to Save Worlds,
Heaven's Gateway, the Vaginal Passage of Peace;
I am blessed with the potential to bring all of us together,
but I need your help.
So come on. Come in,
into the glory of God!
Stick your race into my ethnic melting pot!
Change begins with an act of love!
Change begins in my bedroom!
So let's stop talking about change-
and start fucking for it!


## The View from Gotham
Stacie Boschma

Batman can kiss my ass!
All those nights prowling the streets of Gotham,
and it's still not safe for a woman to walk alone.

I just can't understand how, back in '98,
the city council could spend three million dollars
on that stupid Bat Signal,
but for going on nine months now,
it can't drop three bucks to fix
the streetlight on my corner.

I guess they've given up on crime prevention,
and a taxpayer just has to hope that when shit goes down
that caped crusader is somewhere close,
because 911 sure does take its time these days.

And it is disgusting the way the papers pretend not to know that Batman is Bruce Wayne,
so the city goes on spending our money
when he has plenty, thank you very much.
And if he was such a good citizen, maybe
he could have chipped in for it himself.
My sister down in Metropolis says
Superman never made a dime off of them,
and at least Clark Kent has the decency
to put on some glasses and act
normal when he's not out saving the world.

Not Bruce Wayne though.
That SOB spends his days in the back seats of limousines
buying and selling nations of sweatshops,
while around the world
Wayne Industries bulldozers cart away the rain forests.
The papers say three hundred acres before breakfast, every day.
Every day.

And up here, there isn't enough money
to maintain the parks,
so they're full of tin foil and crack pipes,
and that's just the obvious waste littered beside the human detritus
who sleep in the cold,
hoping Batman doesn't come looking the next time he needs faces to smash
for above-the-fold placement in the morning edition.

Or maybe he just gets bored, just like anyone.
I mean, it's gotta be stressful being Bruce Wayne,
sitting back and watching all that money flow in
between glasses of scotch and snifters of brandy.
So at night he blows off steam by pulling on some tights and trying
to play the hero.
Most guys would just hire a prostitute,
but Mama always said, "Rich people are different."
I swear, if I ever see some giant
bat looking thing come swooping down on me,
he's getting a face full of pepper spray.
I don't care what the papers say,
if you've gotta wear a mask to do good
something ain't right.


## Super Heroes
Joanna Hoffman

Superwoman was a Baltimore waitress.

Delicately balancing scattered ego and scrambled eggs on an overworked wrist twisted
with cysts, and the temptation was strong to throw that tray at the next snarling business-
man to walk into the restaurant, eyes branding her "Stupid dropout" and she wanted to
SCREAM "I HAVE A COLLEGE DEGREE AND I'M A HUMAN BEING, BITCH!" But
Superwoman sharpened her x-ray vision and found that those words, "stupid dropout,"
were etched in her mind, not theirs, and that just like her, all of these customers she
glared at from behind towering trays all carried ketchup-splattered stains of misplaced

insecurity that every ambiguous glance or word seemed to affirm when really, that pain is just a product of one deciding thought, "I'm stupid," and once that spot is wiped clean, it's greaseproof, so Superwoman did what any Superwoman would do: she smiled at them, and meant it, and handed out extra napkins.

Batman was a DC trash man. Beneath sleeping streetlights he took hold of what others had decided to throw away, observing our sloppy cycle of use, lose, repeat, use, lose, repeat, and understanding like only a mortal man could, from his sprawling mansion that could have housed over half the city's homeless to the coldness in his chest that churned out greed like fuel, all these things we think we need and all the things we trash, left out in body bags forming a shameful plastic trail, tossed into the truck as if it were a void canceling out that first spark of existence, as if it were okay to be this wasteful, as if the streets weren't littered with abandoned ghosts, each one lifting up their heads to nod at Batman as he drives by, cementing their unspoken understanding that a message needs to be delivered from these curbside pulpits like a morning sermon, telling the people they can't just press delete and have it all be okay, not when every whitebread breath reverberates in the naked graves of third world countries and Batman knows he can't save the world alone and he refuses to let this city pretend there isn't a world out there to save.

Super hero stories lay scattered in our minds like trading cards, like distant history lessons; once there was a great man named Ghandi, named Martin Luther King; once there was a great woman named Harriet Tubman, named Mother Theresa; and maybe we underestimate just what it takes to be Mother Theresa and maybe we underestimate ourselves by only allowing ourselves to reach for what we can grasp; but super heroes know no limitations, they take a dream, like a collected sigh of relief exhaled throughout the galaxy, and they work towards that, one smile, one breath, one forgiveness at a time.

What is stopping you from being a super hero? What is stopping you from reaching your potential? We've got no excuses. Let's rip off our human skin and levitate, crush evil and fly through walls. I'll be dusting off the earth's throbbing skin to see just how many of you have stopped to check her pulse. Have you? Let me see your hands! See, you're flying, superman! Go out there and be great, not for the fame and the glory but because there's nothing stopping you and what else are you living for? Tattoo your name on the sun, soak up the rain and use it to wash this planet clean. The whole world is waiting for you, so what are you waiting for?

## Web of Trouble
(after Zoolander)
Kevin Bernazzani

I'm falling
backwards down the Empire State Building.
Looking up, I can see the sky.
It feels like I have done this a thousand times.
What made me think I could fly this time?
I'm not Superman.
My life is flashing before my eyes.
I remember my uncle's words:
"With great power, comes great responsibility."

My mind is racing as fast as my body.
So many people are counting on me-
M.J. wanted me at her play tonight;
Aunt May wanted me to help her cook;

Harry was expecting me to go to the Corrib.
But why?
This woman crying in my arms-
why did she call out my name for help?
I'm only an ordinary college student.
I take a deep breath,
then the fear is gone,
I know what I have to do.
I extend my arm,
we gently swing to safety.
The woman whispers in my ear,
"Thank you, Spiderman."

And as she walked away
I thought to myself
"Hey Kevin, haven't you been smoking peyote for six straight days,
and couldn't some of this maybe be in your mind?"
And it was. I was totally fine. I've never even been to New York.


## The Reason We All Want to Be Superman
A.C.Valdez

I think the reason we all want to be Superman isn't because of the strength or the speed or the x-ray vision. It's the black and white. And I don't mean the black and white illustration, I mean the black and white situations, the lack of moral ambiguity, the knowledge that the universe is simply not that complex.

Wouldn't it be nice to live in a world with distinct and uncomplicated good and evil, where we were good and they were bad and if you're not with us, you're against us? Wouldn't it be wonderful if Lex bin-Luthor would just present himself and challenge us "Take me down! The Kryptonite I wield is enough to protect me from you!" And we would outwit him every time?

See, Superman has comics in which he fights Nazis; in which he fights Commies; and other than that, he doesn't bother with International Politics. The Man of Steel has no capacity to deal with the complexities of Vietnam, or Nicaragua, or Grenada, or Panama, or Iraq, or El Salvador, or Israel, or Palestine, or any other place that violates his world's simple black and white. And isn't that nice?


## Super-Power
Rich Macklin

If I could have any superpower, what would I have?
If I could be any super hero, who would I be?

Would I be invisible? Or have x-ray vision? No, more often than that, those fantasies are less about heroism, and more about the adolescent sort of fantasy...and with internet porn and a girlfriend, I can see the naked female form easy enough.

Would I have super-strength? No, if I did, it would just be buying into some sort of macho stereotype. Heck, if I want to smash something, I can buy a hammer. If I want to open something, I can buy a crowbar. If I want to lift something, I'll get the jack from my car.

Would I be able to fly? Well, that would be cool. It could get me to the scene of the crime or disaster easily, but what could I do when I get there?

No, if I was a super hero, I would have to take the Bodhisattva route. I'd have to sacrifice. I would even have to sacrifice in a way that didn't seem cool to be sacrificial. Not the altar blood crazy sacrifice, nor the martyr, with all of its romantic pain.

If I could be any super hero, I would have to be the boring super hero. I would be the least cool, but most helpful super hero of all. I would be...I would be...

Incredibly Persuasive Man!

Not Brainwashing Man, because that would be a supervillain. Not My-Way-Or-The-High-way Man, because then I would be a superjerk. I would just be the most persuasive man ever. I would convince people to change their mind with the ease that Superman can fly or Aquaman can swim.

Think of it, think of it...

I could convince Starbucks to sell all their locations to cool people who could have art openings and poetry readings.

I could convince Nike and Gap and all those companies to pay living wages, and I could convince the masses that a Swoosh or a Name doesn't make a garment better.

I could end wars, get the rich to help the poor, I could do this because I could convince the gatekeepers to let me in to talk to all the wealthy people who normally know enough to have gatekeepers, lest they be convinced to use their money for better things.

I could even convince TV studios and publishers to hire me to convince people, and that way I'd be the only super hero that actually gets an income, so I wouldn't be stealing things like the Justice League always did. Excuse me, borrow. Yeah.

I would be wonderful.

But it would be as stressful as battling aliens and robots. With great power comes great responsibility, and I'd have to read a lot about things so I knew what I was talking about. I'd have to convince teachers and scholars and Zen masters and peacemakers to teach me what they would teach everyone, if only they were incredibly persuasive man.

...and I wouldn't get to wear spandex or armor. Heck, I'd probably have to wear a suit sometimes.


# Super Hero?
Bruce Gordon

> "*Super hero - a person of unprecedented physical prowess dedicated to acts of darring-do in the public interest.*"
>
> -Michael Chabon

I wrote this quote down last year about this time. I was in Florida (I detest Florida), for my father's funeral (I liked my father), avoiding my mother by reading (I'm that fond of her). I was thinking about the concept of a wholly real person who does un-real actions that benefit people kind- with style. It was going to be called the "Gay Super

Hero." No capes or tights, just fantastic actions, with panache. The big idea was to have these people proclaimed on my web site with reasons as to why they were nominated and what their accomplishments were. That was the plan. I then had a crippling case of insecurity.

I asked myself, "Self, what do you know of super heroes? C'mon, you grew up in a time when most heroes were soon corpses; and you came of age at a time when all your heroes were poets and musicians with great hair and rubber O-rings on their wrists!" This is where I stopped, looked around and took stock of people I have lived amongst. Actually, at the time I was rather forced to as I was sitting in the "family room," and every inch of wall space was covered with framed collages of family members. There was even a photo of my father, in a collage, showing a collage picture to someone. Kinda creepy.

My parents, I thought, would make pretty good super heroes. Their superpower would be "extreme perseverance in extreme situations." That's what I've divined from the many stories I've been told and ones I've been privy to. The things they have done, for others and for us kids have been just phenomenal. Of course, no one retires to Florida without helping themselves a bit, but on the whole, there are at least two generations of folks who are thankful for them.

And beyond all this, I still wrestle with the concept of super heroes. Put simply, my heroes are all human and based in reality. Even the super ones amongst them are, or were, people that I have known. One may not have seen them in the funny papers or newsreels, but their impact has been profound. I could talk about these folks for pages: which would be a Herculean task in itself...and I've got other feats of derring-do to do.

Since I'm the son-o'-super heroes, I have my own superpower. It is the ability "to accept and understand the universe as it is." I wield this power to help folks to see and experience as many sides of reality as they can. I have a load of tools to employ: tarot and divination; love; Qabbalah; astrology; intuition; observation; psychology; deduction and reasoning; knowledge and truths; music and a dangerous memory to boot. It seems that many people can only relate to what their five senses tell them. I always aver that there is more, much more, but folks have to be taught how to experience the universe as an adventure and not a burden. Because of this, some call me "reverend." Some call me other things or other names and one six year old calls me "grandfather." I'm not her grandfather in the usual sense, but that's the name she gave me and I revel in it. Why argue with a six year old? One person cursed me with the title of "Living Archivist," which sorrowfully describes my apparent longevity.

Whatever my title, I try my best to aid folks in their tribulations. I try to help people by giving them any tools they need to experience their universe without fear, without hate and without mendacity. I help people find hope. Is that so different from comic book heroes? I think not.

## My Secret Super Hero Powers
Karen Garabrant

I envy the powers of the clairvoyant, with green crystal balls, dream catchers, and funky, dried talismans. Maybe if we could see the ghosts haunting each other's third eyes, we would see each other more clearly with the other two. I think it would be cool to place my hands on books, running palms up and down spines, sucking up the content from between the lines in my fingerprints, up my arm, and into my head. I love rolling around in language, but, when time is short, sometimes I need to know, by touch, what a book has inside.

These are my super hero thoughts as the media drones on about powers made necessary by 9/11: the compression of events, the implosion of buildings, two metal fingers where one-plus-one, made eleven, then suddenly made Ground Zero. I dare the tv to brainwash me. I think about super hero powers like the strength to see through flags and see through flags and see light on the other side, not eye-for-an-eye, not this vile-vengeful-violence rhetoric of war.

Because I fear the arrogance of masculinity combined with authority; of the triumph and the will. I profile men that terrorize me the most. I base this on abuse stories and the loopholes as white as scott-free tissue. I want to be the super hero with the power to remember history. I want this power to suck the horror out, bury it under eternal flame, and call the cycle over. I want the super power of the Arthurian Princess in flowing skirts and glittery skin with her hand held out, as in, "the circle of violence stops here."

Once upon a time, it made sense to want to be a cop-detective because I loved the Bionic Woman, Charlie's Angels, and Wonder Woman. Later, fascinated by burning things, I wanted to know how fire worked and wanted to be a fire woman who could start them (Poof! Fire!) and put them out, (Poof! Smoke!) The boys in my neighborhood didn't dare say I couldn't 'cause I was a girl- I owned half their matchbox cars.

Today, I think of the word play of bumper stickers and I'd like to whirl some peas and feed the world: I'd like to be the strange-visitor-as-dove, hypnotizing the war mongers into surrendering to world peace. I'd be Mother Earth In Microcosm. But, I know: my secret super power will always be in the pen in my pocket with the sidekick of paper. My secret super hero power is cutting commemorative flags, my power cuts through the pomp, and the propaganda.

My power will be pens that won't go away My power is to cut through the trite even as I write it now. My secret super hero power is to record the ordinary as the super reality of our common language. The real super powers come back to the truth of human faces trying to figure out how do we all survive, together?

## Lost & Found in Tromaville
Eric ZORK Alan

I was lost.

"More limbs- get more limbs in there!" Lloyd screams.

Terry, the script supervisor, sworn to continuity of details, says, "But Lloyd, you have three shots in the can that won't match."

"Thank you for your input, Terry, but this is Tromaville," Lloyd says.
Terry starts, "But Lloyd, my job is..."

"More limbs. It's Tromaville! Get some hands... and a few heads!"

For the overhead shot there simply has to be more carnage...this is a Troma picture after all- there are standards of carnage to be upheld. And, in Tromaville, there really is no such thing as continuity. Lloyd aims above the details.

Lloyd Kaufman is one of those truly brilliant people. It's not just that he is a Harvard or Yale graduate. It's not just that he built an incredibly successful business. It's just that he is Lloyd - part maniac, part philosopher and the rest only God knows what. He's a man that can yell really loud if it suits his fancy. But he can also talk about Nietzsche. If he is a maniac, he certainly is a charming one.

Moments ago, we blew up a house.

Running around like a madman I hand out 100 earplugs. Speaking with a strange Swedish accent (don't ask), I repeat to all on set: "Earplugs for big bang- big, big boom!" I never needed earplugs before, but when you blow up a house it is a good idea. Trust me.

It's my first day on set. My first major motion picture. This is what I went to school for- to help blow up buildings and get more body parts inside the circle of thugs trying to kill the mutated super-hero from New Jersey. Toxic Avenger Part II- if you are truly cultured, then you know what I'm talking about- if not, maybe you should expand your horizons.

Troma changed my life. It was a long time ago- I always knew I wanted to work in movies. With a degree in Broadcast & Film from Boston University, I hit the New York pavement knocking on every door trying to get work on some boring commercial as a geeky gopher. That was what film graduates did. But, I loved movies. I mean, I LOVE movies!!

A couple days after the explosion we are shooting in a park in Peekskill. I am standing around waiting to be told to fetch this or that. Lloyd yells, "Zork, go sit on the steps over there and, you know, look homeless." It's been a bad casting day, things are way behind schedule, and in Tromaville that is normal but just won't do, so Lloyd sends me in with a local lady to fill up the shot.

Set locked, slate slapped. Camera rushes in and Lloyd says, "Zork, say something."

"What should I say, Lloyd?"

"I don't know, anything. Say, "Mom, who are these people?" OK, roll camera."

Flustered and confused, I blurt out five simple words.

"Let's get one for safety," Lloyd says. I repeat my line.

"Cut. Print. Wrap. Let's move on, we're losing the light."

Right then and there Lloyd made me a movie star. Minutes before I had been an unknown bumbling Production Assistant, and now I had my five seconds of fame. A year later Mario Van Peebles would say the same thing to me on a completely different shoot. "Zork, get over there and look homeless." I hoped it was just a symptom of not combing my hair enough and not foreshadowing. I was sure one day film scholars would appreciate the subtle nuances of my Troma performance. But at that moment it was time to get back to my PA duties.

I must have been mad when I went to work for Troma. Months before that madness, after my first job offer for a commercial, I had called them:

Troma man on the phone says, "You don't want to work here!"

"Yes, I do," I say.

"Trust me, you don't. We work you like a dog and yell at you a lot. REALLY, you don't want to work here!"

"Whatever doesn't kill me makes me stronger- and I used to have a cat." I say.

"We pay you next to nothing. You DON'T want to work here."

"Art rarely pays. I DO want to work for Troma."

We fought about this for some time- I won. Troma had really odd recruiting methods. For 12 weeks, 6 days a week, 16 hours a day I was immersed in Tromaville. Dickens wrote about a best of times/worst of times scenario. I am sure he must have worked for Troma.

But mostly, it was the best of times. If you didn't mind bypassing the luxuries of normal life like sleep, sex and a firm financial foundation, then Tromaville was a great place to live, for a while.

I have daily duties on the shoot. I am the go-getter PA, and every time the "good people of Tromaville" are needed, I rub dirt on my face, put on a stupid hat, and get in front of the camera.

Frequently I get beat up with a loaf of bread- by Spawn. Actually, Michael Jai White and, as a running gag, every chance he gets, he takes the loaf of bread I have in my shopping cart and hits me over the head. How many people can say they have been beaten up with loafs of bread by Spawn?

And I get to watch Arthur, the lucky British FX guy, paint a lovely naked lady. I am not sure why she has to be naked or why she is adorned with illustrations, but I can hardly say I object. And, after all, this is Tromaville. I want Arthur's job.

 In between shots I hang out with my fellow PA's. Here I am with Kuzy- I love her- that smile- what's right behind those eyes- I have never told her, I have never kissed her. Certain dreams are better off left that way. Then, they can stay with you forever.

In a few seconds, I have to run down the street to pick up a dozen pizzas. These film crews get pretty unruly if you don't feed them.

Snap back to present day- the here and ho-hum now. I program computers for more money, but I haven't gotten to blow up any houses recently, Spawn hasn't beaten me up with French bread in almost a decade, and I never order more than one pizza at a time. But ten years ago I lived in Tromaville, I was in love, and I was a movie star.

I am found. (Thanks Troma.)


## Stan Jablonski: Zombie Hunter
Michael Whalen

When there's no more room in HELL the dead will
walk the EARTH.
And on that glorious, glorious day,
Stan Jablonski will be a man!

When the former United States is inexplicably overrun
by hordes of the walking dead, an ungodly obscenity so
foul it rivals the coffee at my office, and Alaska is
annexed by Canada, and Hawaii is obliterated by
Godzilla and Rodan, and there is no hope for outside
help, Stan Jablonski will rise above.

He will roam the countryside in his fantasy art
airbrushed tractor trailer hauling a Winnebago hauling
a wood-chipper, beckoned by the monotonous collective
moans of "brains brains brains." And as the
townspeople and villagers begin to hear the haunted
voices slowly die off one by one, they will know that
it is Stan Jablonski reducing the choir to
disconnected soloists.

Now, I'm not one to use the term "Magnificent Undead
Corpse Grinding Bastard" loosely, but if ever a man
deserved such a title, it'd be Stan Jablonski. He will
master the essential survival skills of the
apocalypse; like how to siphon gasoline, hot-wire a
car, make grackle jerky, and place a bullet between
the eyes of a very slowly moving target at 300 yards!
He'll be like the Johnny Appleseed of zombie
destruction, liberating towns and practicing finishing
lines like, "I'll see you in Hell, Stinky…"

In the heartland of America, fathers will open their
zombie-proof cellars and ask Stan to protect their
beautiful daughters, to which he'll respond, "My
apologies, sir, but I've only come here to do two
things: decapitate zombies and pillage comic book
stores, and your shit-ass town ain't got no comic book
stores."

Because the post-zombie apocalypse will be a
collector's paradise! All you've ever desired, there
for the taking! An entire doomed landscape of "Finders
keepers; losers brains eaten!"

Not only will Stan Jablonksi have a copy of Amazing
Fantasy #15, the first appearance of Spider-Man,
but he'll have 427 copies! His tractor trailer, a
roving Mylar-protected comics library, will be the
stuff of geek legend!

In the newfound freedom of this immoral anarchy, one
of Stan's secret vices will be to hunt down his
childhood bullies, kill them, wait six hours for their
resurrection, and kill them again. A small price to
pay for freedom from terror, I say.

In the future, Stan Jablonski may be rolling into your
town, dropping monsters into wood-chippers, and
looting comic book stores.

But until that opportunistic sign of the apocalypse
arrives, Mrs. Jablonksi, Stanley needs to turn his
homework in on time, change out of his sweatpants, and
comb his hair, otherwise he will not graduate 8th
grade and he will never, ever get a date to the cotillion.

## El Fantastico Nino Volador/The Fantastic Flying Boy
Adriana Ramirez

Chapultepec

These stairs spill marrow like light beams.
He wraps himself, cradled, in a flag,
climbs till stars become dome-strokes,
and prepares to fly.

He rises torch in hand,
memory bleeding, forgotten.

Mujeres Invisibles/Invisible Women

Juarez

Dotted lines spring to life,
sprouting guard booths & machine gun bridges.
She dons vines and fruits,
ascends into moss and river water.
Her angels soak her smothered
screams in plastic rings and hang themselves
with halos

Las Sombras/The Shadows

Arizona

We hold our breath for a minute, men
With guns raise dust clouds.
We fade into covers
like deathbed prayers.
Comforted,
we seek water and salvation. The desert
births us: we are now suns and scars.


## We Have Met the Enemy
Frank Miller

" *We have met the enemy and they is us.*"

- Walt Kelly.


After all we were just plain and decent folk,
quite powerless to halt this flow of blood;
decent, yes, and quite ordinary - this flood
of pain, of death - not ours. This - soak
of, excuse me, shit and bile - not our doing -
not our doing - we could not be at fault.
We turned our heads away from this assault
upon our decency knowing that not viewing
would leave us then untainted by this guilt.
Others must take the blame for we are clean,
untouched by filth and sewage stink and silt.
We do not understand. What do you mean
by accusations? There was no crime; not one
and being none it cannot be undone.

## Dr. God
Melissa Guillet

In the beginning,
it was Mendel who had meddled
in pea pods large and tall.

"It's a wonderful life,"
Gould would say
of trilobites and evolution.

Soon, there were sheep
without mothers, ears
on the backs of mice,
pairs of cells pulsating
in synchronized hearts.

We create our gods
in our own image:
Durer's self-portrait as Jesus;
Dante's friends in high places.

And now the doctor holds God
in his hands.
On the altar, the tools are laid:
a cell, a syringe, a centrifuge.

They say he is creating monsters.
They say he is Dr. Moreau.
But his converts give their eggs,
and the stem cell secrets continue.

Balancing on the scales
is a sermon of ethics and science.
The centrifuge spins
like Russian roulette:
Replacement organs, altered humans,
X-Men and Generation Y.

We are the creators of gods.
What will we replace ourselves with?


## Captain America Writes Home
John Powers

The first thing I will tell you
is, NO MORE FLEA COLLARS.
That huge misinformation item is actually harmful
and causes skin rashes, nausea, and potentially nervous disorders.

Here we have treated uniforms for insect protection,
and we're trained on how to stay bug free.
The flea collar issue is the remnant of some old time special forces grunt attitude.

That does not work.
Special forces grunts are idiots.
Don't listen to them.

Don't listen to your father, either.
We do not need lawn sprinklers.
The grass can wait until I get home.
If it's brown you won't have to mow.

Baby wipes are good,
especially since we often run out of toilet paper,
and some areas the guys can go a week or more
without a shower.
Baby wipes.

We all like beef jerky,
Peanut M&Ms are a premium item here...
very hard to find.

Dark socks really suck,
they turn your toes black.
I only wear white cotton socks.
I have about 50 pairs now,
but keep 'em coming!
I'll give them away.

Just about any non-issue uniform item is not authorized,
so no more scarves,
fluffy hats; stuff like that is a NO GO.
Thank Jilly though.

Nearly every soldier in the theater
is issued Wiley X sunglasses that have ballistic glass lenses,
so cheap sunglasses really do nobody any good.
Thanks though.

What I really like is when someone gets a box full of NEWSWEEK,
Sports Illustrated magazines,
new issues of Batman.
That's what I really like.
I get yesterday's news tomorrow,
but at least I can read something
that's not the Stars and Stripes.
Say 'Hi' to the kids.
Don't tell Dad,
but we voted for Kerry.

- Winning hearts and minds,

Your Husband

## Mutant Ninja Turtle Boy
Ray McNiece

The end is not near, but it is near here-
the backside of Worcester, a cold, gray version
of the last days of Pompeii, a rain of used junk
and discount store packaging having settled
in layers between peeling triple deckers
surrounded by freeways encircling Indian Lake.
Inside, Mom has given up on Judgment Day
for a better show on TV. She's trying to stretch
groceries till her next government check.
Her old man finally quit his job shoveling crap
against the tide and split to the land of deadbeat Dads.

"Hey Mister," says her son, wearing a dirty
mutant ninja turtle T-shirt, shivering arms
pulled inside sleeves so elbows stump out,
"Hey Mister," his eyes floundering on one side
of his face, teeth jutting every way but straight,
blue pie or impetigo, or a bruise on his cheek,
"Hey Mister, wanna play war?" flipper pointing
to a pile of monsters and soldiers on hardpan yard.

How many more plastic action figures need to be
molded before the scales shift and critical mass
spills, and the world becomes more garbage than
product, more product than raw material, more
material than spirit? God Money counts the good
of another gross of mutant ninja turtles,
the jobs they provide, the trickle down effect,
like the spit running from the boy's mouth
as he begs again, "Hey Mister, wanna play war?"

## Voltron vs. the Universe
J. Bradley

some days, i think i'm Voltron
fistfuls of particles ready to forge the blazing sword
and strike down Ro-Beasts rampaging across the galaxy
except i got Lance and Princess Aurora
in the fists
Pidge and Keith
in the feet
and Hunk at the helm:

i speak before thinking
and shortly after acting.
afterwards, i suck on my foot
for a mouthful of hindsight;
that's just on a good day.

the universe is collapsing,
pop-up landscapes swallowed by the maw of God
as disjointed paper angels try joining hands
to finally fly home.

what does this have to do with Voltron?
everything.
what does this have to do with me?
not enough.

if i was Voltron,
i'd wrap these mighty arms around
crazed ex-girlfriends disguised
as hurricanes
and leave them where stars are too fat
for their own geometry,
ready to blossom into fractal patterns
and burn the ceiling,
then burst back through the atmosphere
and bring the fear to Prince Lotor.

if i was Voltron,
i'd stop steel love bugs
ripe with fuel and life
from mating with buildings
and spawning still born children
made of industrial glass,
charred skin, and the dusty breath
of collapse.
once done, i'd pose with a gleam in my eye
before taking to the sky, as intact innocents
wave goodbye.
if i was Voltron,
i'd tear time and space asunder
and return minutes before a cracked o-ring
unlocked the surly bonds of earth
and unleashed slivers of a second sun
to undo the moment
Ms. Mack's first graders
lost a little piece of wonder.

but i'm no Voltron.

i've got a neck like silly putty,
a heart palpitating in whispers,
arms confused about what shade of white
they should be
and feet that beat like upstairs neighbors fucking
in retreat.  combined, i'm the embodiment
my mother raised me to be: lower class America
crafting a middle class life from coupons
and rounded corners.

these hands
won't build towers of babble on soapbox stanzas so high
anyone could climb to the top and see if there was a God
and if there was, point out to him
since he made us in his image,
no wonder why our existence
is so fucked up.

these eyes
tire of banking our recovery
on self-righteous celebrities,
people who forgot the impact of the words
"struggle," "tragedy," "poverty"
asking folks like me
to open their wallets and their hearts
while barraging us with shell game ideology,
noting four days after
Kanye had the balls to say
George W. Bush hates black people,
Jesus himself blessed that man
with album sales of just under 900,000.

but that's just Hunk at the helm again.

i can taste the 'what if's' and 'should've dones'
on the roof of my mouth
but i'm too human and not enough noble
to let rent checks skate on lakes
of below zero balances, declare laundry days
national holidays, practice pyrokinesis
on past due power bills.

my redemption will be in my future children,
who i hope lead me by their example
and put their old man to shame one day.

i feel like Voltron
sometimes-
fistfuls of particles
aching to forge the blazing sword
that could save the world
one slain Ro-Beast at a time;
that's just on a good day.


## Look!  In the Sky!
Kevin Covall

3rd world
in Spain
the unnamable
untouchable
invisible
whiteMAN

able to steal small countries in a single bond
whiteMAN wears 10-gallon hats of oxygen
whiteMAN  is the son of famous forefathers
    faces carved into Rushmore, generations of oil/slave $$
whiteMAN is always w(R)ight/man
    stop asking
        Alexander Graham Bell is a white MAN so
whiteMAN  makes unlimited phone calls to bank baron hotlines
whiteMAN is a daredevil sending puppets to barrios and ghettos at rent time
whiteMAN's Cadillac is parked in the sky just out of reach of children's dreams
whiteMAN is a speeding bullet aimed at justifiable homicide
        hi-Oh Sliver away!!!!!!!!!!! (from international tribunals)
            THE HAUGE!!!!!!!!!!!!!!!!
        by day whiteMAN is a one-eyed reporter for The Gotham Daily
            a mild-mannered public school principal
                writing Columbus into curriculum
            a billionaire bachelor hiding maids in the basement
            an out-sourced union laborer mad at Mexicans
            a leading hollywood Christian Scientist
                protesting the ban of anal beads
                by coming out
                with a line of anal beads
    available at fine department stores
    by night whiteMAN
            throws bodies of color off the decks of yacht parties
        democracies behind close door cigar smoke
whiteMAN spreads Coke-a-Cola(c) like a virus  MTV
    humpty dumpty empty memory eggshell erasure programs
whiteMAN buttwipes finger/foot prints from the land
whiteMAN's  superpower is NO MEMORY
      forget a people here, whiteMAN walks alone for three seconds
          claims discovery
          sticks his pole into the soil
          populates space w/ whiteMEN
          he teeth light the sky / smile big as the milky way
whiteMAN is the brother of G-d's son
    heaven's gatekeeper
    sole proprietor of the only game in town
whiteMAN won the wild west
    climbed Mt. Everest(tm)
    mounted Miss Universe(c)
whiteMAN faster than a swarm of locusts
    Ebola
    3-legged leper races
whiteMAN is awesome dude!
    tubular!
    radicalllll!
      rollingstonebeatle soundtracks bumpinnnnnn
      Darwin dude! Darwin fuckin rocks!
whiteMAN a real american hero
      an international superstar
      history in the making
      a man we'll read about
        for ages

## Post-Katrina Super Heroes We'd Love to See
(a haiku sequence)
Kasandra Larsen

I. THE MASKED ADJUSTER

Freak, born with a heart,
he rides at night, bringing checks
and hope to thousands.

II. MAYOR THE MAGNIFICENT

Endowed with huge balls!
Vision! Brains! And a talent
for resurrection.

II. THE MYSTICAL FLYING CHEF

Miss home? He'll appear
with crawfish, beignets, gumbo,
and a pecan pie.

IV. THE FABULOUS FEMA FIVE

This team comes prepared:
food, water, tents, medicine,
buses- and a plan.

V. THE INCREDIBLE AMSTERDAM DYKE

Stronger than steel,
tough, tall, massive. That green Hulk?
No match for this bitch.


## Legion of Doom
Daphne Gottlieb

We only get the super heroes
we can imagine, never
the ones we need.
We don't need more
super heroes, just better ones,
say the idealists.

Third-world Marxists say,
If we build a super hero, she will be nothing
like Wonder Woman.
There is so much wrong
with Wonder Woman:
She is white when

most of the world isn't. She has a jet
which is a gas-guzzler, usurping resources
that might better serve the people.

You're wrong, say the feminists.
You're missing what is really wrong
with Wonder Woman, how her body

type is unsustainable
for most women and it is unhealthy
how she is put on display

in a see-thru jet, the Fredrick's of Hollywood
of air travel, a 360-degree glass ceiling
that moves as fast as she does

and another thing -- no one makes
Aquaman run
in four-inch heels, and --

Fighting crime is still fighting, say the pacifists.  No fighting.
You are shortsighted, say the militants.
You are missing the point, say the post-colonialists.

Oh yeah? say the Promise Keepers.
A woman's place is --
Who let YOU in? ask the lesbian separatists.

It comes to blows quickly, over a question
of who is the most wrong
and everyone has forgotten altogether

about Wonder Woman,
who has slipped out
through the back

of the discussion,
as invisible
as her jet.
How to save the world this time?
She tosses her bullet-deflecting bracelets
and her golden lasso

into the trash
and leaves her super headband
perched on top, shining dully.

She is too tired.
Let them damn well fight
their own damned crime.


## Secret Identity
Cecilia Tan

They believe in freedom, they believe in justice
Leagues and legions, teams of titans
Sometimes they work in pairs
Some work
alone

Though the world needs saving, every now and then
Comes a quiet time, the waiting
What do super heroes
do when on
vacation?

When you've got super speed, and super reflexes
And computers the size of a room
You can play a lot
of games on
Nintendo

## Boudicca
Valerie Lawson

She was heroic, dangerous, goddess-like
With grizzled carroty hair and a temper to match.
She lifted me from baby-fat safety, taught me
How to run through the woods, screaming
Like a banshee or quiet, without snapping a twig.
We were blue-faced Celts draped in pagan oak,
Native Americans before they were called that.
In our games, there were no Cowboys, no Roman
Armies, just green essence.

We pretended not to hear the calls for supper
And civilization. Home meant having the dirt scrubbed off,
Tick checks and hair curlings, dresses in place of
Dungarees, chafing in the smallness of rooms.

She taught me how to ride, bareback,
Because that's the way it should be done.
She knew that horsed, the world was ours.
Our range extended a day's ride
On an abandoned set of railroad tracks
Rusting toward its mirage point.

Boudicca rode tall on a leopard spot
Appaloosa, I followed along everywhere,
Tonto, Sancho, on the much smaller,
If no less magnificent painted pony.
We smoked and laughed out loud.
Liberated piglets from the neighbor's farm.
Went on mad divot gallops across the local golf course
Defying the illusion of that open space.

All the while, the Roman Legions advanced,
Built walls and Empires. We huddled in her cramped
Room on rainy days, listened to wobbly forty-fives,
The Monkees, Tom Jones, Carole King,
You make me feel like a natural woman...
Why, why, why, Delilah? Another Pleasant Valley...
Incomplete aliens, we slid along the margins
Of the walking world. The Indians disappeared.

Boudicca got married, had babies, sold her horses,
hung up her sword, wrapped her armor in tissue paper,
and boxed it in the attic. The iron rails were hauled away,
Smelted down for scrap. The painted pony died.
Though I could ride backward, light a cigarette
Or drink a can of Pepsi on the back of a galloping horse
I could not hold on to the edge of this earth.
I would never be that tall again.
The spark I hold onto is a daughter. She is heroic,
Dangerous, and has the most brilliant red highlights in her hair.
Warrior child, choose your mount wisely
And god speed. Boudicca rides again.

## Super Ho
Tony Brown

About the name: she came up with it
in an off moment. Not that she liked the label,
or thought it applied to her or anyone else, really;
but after years of being ogled by teenagers
who caught her in mid-flight all spangled and
skintight, after selling her image
to the pinball and video game merchants,
after trying to make a living fighting crime
and only getting noticed for tits and ass,
it only took a last-straw leer and a bad joke
to make it stick in her head for good.

She thought about changing the costume to Juicy Couture,
changing the persona to soccer mom from another planet, modern woman
bitten by a radioactive feminist spider -- eh. Stick with
the tried and true, she decided, and let the bastards
think what they want. I'll keep at it my way,
maybe kick more balls than ass for awhile
just to make them a little more wary of what they think.

Soon enough, she started skipping the super hero meetings.
She cropped her hair
and stopped talking to Iron Man, that condescending prick.
She never went by the bar anymore, missing out on
the locker-room jokes and tips for dealing with
parallel universes -- hell, she thought, I'm in a parallel universe
every time I step into a room with these jokers.

On a cold day on October she hung up the leotard for the last time.

These days she sits around a lot. She uses her powers sparingly --
turning back time, for example, to get to the video store before it closes.
She watches a lot of movies and wishes she was Katherine Hepburn, sometimes,
but mostly she's happy -- takes lovers when she chooses
but more often sleeps alone and loves it, lets the catalogs pile up untouched,
and never, ever, thinks of her name.

# Another Day in Paradise
Ed Fuqua

She still reads comic books, but she never goes to the chat rooms anymore.
the comic was bad enough, but it seemed like good public relations,
at the time. And that's what really counts
when you're Ambassador, and you have a message
that no one in man's world wants to hear.

It's not like admitting she was a lesbian
would really hurt sales of the comic.
They practically spell it out anyway,
anyone over the age of twelve
who reads the origin already knows.
Did they really expect people to buy the whole Steve Trevor thing?
Don't get me wrong, Steve was a great guy. Diana really liked him.
But her first lover had been over two thousand years old,
she had sweated and bled on the plains of Troy, and had taken women
by the shores of the Black Sea, while their castrated
husbands bled to death. Of course the writers always leave that part out.

It was like those Justice League meetings, Black Canary shifting
uncomfortably in her chair. She was the one wearing fishnets
and high heels. She expected the guys to look.
But not Diana. Oh. no, that would violate the unwritten rules.
Only Superman and Batman really felt comfortable around her.
They weren't intimidated, and they had nothing to prove.
When They would sit around the Fortress Of Solitude,
sometimes Superman would say something like,
"Lois doesn't understand me."
And Diana would nod her head as if she understood.

She still laughs when she reads the stories with bondage
and S&M in them. It's always funny when men try to wrap their minds
around ideas that are beyond them. They've never worn the bracelets;
they've never been bound by a man.

It was like the time she was fighting the Cheetah,
and she had thrown Diana to the floor and was on top of her,
razor sharp claws an inch from her throat. Diana just looked at her
and said, "Why don't you just admit what we're both feeling?"
and that was all it took,
another super villain down.

Diana put down the comic book. On the grass next to her,
the Cheetah rolls over on her back, stretching
in the afternoon sun.
There is the sound of clashing steel. A few yards away
two Amazons fight. They are naked,
like all Greek athletes. Diana watches them
and feels the Cheetah's coarse tongue trace a circle
on her shoulder blade. Fingers begin kneading her muscles,
those muscles that could crush brick, deflect bullets,
make a lover sigh with ecstasy.

Maybe the comic would sell better
if they told the whole story.
Maybe.
But there are some things that people just never understand.


## Wonder Woman Dreams of the Amazon
Jeannine Gailey

I miss the tropes of Paradise's green vines
roped around wrists, jasmine coronets,
the improbable misty clothing of my tribe.

I dream of the land of my birth. They named
me after their patron Goddess.
I was to be a warrior for their kind.

I miss my mother, Hippolyta.
In my dreams she wraps me tightly
again in the American flag,
warning me,
            "Cling to your bracelets,
your magic lasso. Don't be a fool for men."

She's always lecturing me, telling me
not to leave her. Sometimes she changes
into a doe, and I see my father
shooting her, her blood. Sometimes,
in these dreams, it is me who shoots her.

My daily transformation
from prim kitten-bowed suit to bustier
with red-white-and-blue stars
is less complicated. The invisible jet
makes for clean escapes.
The animals are my spies and allies;
inexplicably, snow-feathered doves
appear in my hands. I capture Nazis
and Martians with boomerang grace.
When I turn and turn, the music plays louder,
the glow around me burns white-hot,
I become everything I was born to be,
the dreams of the mother,
the threat of the father.


## Female Comic Book Super Heroes
Jeannine Gailey

are always fighting evil in a thong,
pulsing techno soundtrack in the background
as their tiny ankles thwack
against the bulk of male thugs.

With names like Buffy, Elektra, or Storm,
they excel in code decryption, Egyptology, and pyrotechnics.
They pout when tortured, but always escape just in time,
still impeccable in lip gloss and pointy-toed boots,
to rescue male partners, love interests, or fathers.
Impossible chests burst out of tight leather jackets,
from which they extract the hidden scroll or antidote,
tousled hair covering one eye.

They return to their day jobs as forensic pathologists,
wearing their hair up, donning dainty glasses.
Of all the goddesses, these pneumatic heroines most
resemble Artemis, with her miniskirts and crossbow,
or Freya, with her giant gray cats.
Each has seen this apocalypse before.
See her perfect three-point landing on top of the chariot,
riding the silver moon into the horizon,
city crumbling around her heels.


## Mawate
(for Harper & Joy)
Jen Mahon

In Japanese, "mawate" means "to turn oneself around".

The martial arts are balanced motion poetry,
fists and feet moving fluid and free.

It is more than metaphor when a blackbelt
places her fist against my abdomen, and tells me to
move through it.

Mawate. Turn Around.

And the obstacle I move through is more than her hand,
so steady and strong against my center.
I move through every hand
placed on me against my will.
I move through eyes staring
at hips and breasts and thighs.
I move through rape after rape
after rape of sisters, friends, lovers,
self.

Mawate.  Turn around.

My sensei tells me to
breathe,
move,
step.

And I do, inch by aching inch,
turn heel,
slide foot,
turn heel,
slide foot,
turn heel,
breathe,
move.
I move through more in those three steps,
with her fist clenched
against my body,
than years of therapy can get me through.

                                    Mawate.  Turn around.
                    I am a martial artist because I refuse to be the weaker sex.
                    I am a martial artist so I can set boundaries and hold them.
                        I am a martial artist with the word "warrior"
                                        imbued in my movements.
                                I am shedding the skin of victim.
                    I am reclaiming every ounce of flesh ever stolen from me
                                            with flung words,
                                            leered looks,
                                            and groping hands.
                            I am finally grasping my own skin,
                                starting with my fists and arms,
                                breasts, breath, and belly,
                                        hips and thighs.
                                Grasping my own skin.
                                Grasping my own skin.
                                Grasping on my own skin
                                            and pulling.

Mawate.  Turn around.

Each time I sink cinder-fingered fists into heavy bags,
feeling weight reverberate,
I rebalance myself,
repossess another fiber, another cell.

Each time I move through the patterns of kata,
I reshape the patterns of my expectations.

Every time I step into the dojo,
throw a punch, a kick, a nukite, a shote,
a uraken,
or take a breath,
I stand shoulder
to shoulder
to shoulder
with women
for whom "survivor" is not a strong enough word,
women who will accept no less than the word "warrior".

Mawate.  I am turning myself around.

# Thunder Girl
Jill Binder

It happened in the bookstore.  I was
incognito as usual—
the standard glasses disguise really does work best.
He noticed me, black hair up in a bun, brown skirt suit,
attitude of a tigress taking a brief rest.
Charmed by my electricity, he knocked a pile of books over.

I could have easily blasted them back into place
with a snap of my fingers,
but no, that would have violated
so many regulations in the Codex of Conduct.
Besides, it was charming when Brian-
(short, stocky, nervous like a pug)-
insisted on putting them back, a little clumsily.

I chuckled, thinking about how just the night before,
I had single-handedly saved the city yet again
from Dr. Nefarious and his ten Horrendous Henchmen,
before they took out the hydro and filled everybody's homes with noxious gases.

Being lesser-known among my kind,
It's always entertaining to catch them by surprise,
foil their plans
with a little strategically-placed hail and lightning,
before engaging in a bit of one-on-group
hand-to-hand combat.
Fighting like a master chess player,
knocking out pawns on every move.

Above all, in my heart of hearts,
my cherished part: making the grand
entrance- a mini storm full of flash and dazzle,
then I emerge, landing catlike on my
feet. Hands on hips, always taking a moment
to take a stern look around.
Assessing the scene, as my blue, shimmering cape
dances on air behind me.
What can I say? Like my colleagues,
I'm all about dramatic flair

I said yes to coffee with Brian the next day.
It had been a while since I'd dated,
busy with my double-life and all.
He was endearing: opening doors for me,
getting our coffee, offering my coat.

As we dated, I re-experienced things I hadn't done in a while;
riding in a car instead of flying-
going to a movie instead of whipping up
a little light storm in my backyard.

When he moved in, I had never let myself
get that close to a mundane before.
The most difficult part was keeping
my Thunder Girl identity secret.

There were close calls—
like the time Snakehead followed me home,
then surrounded the house with his army
of humanoid reptiles. Fortunately,
Brian was out of town for a conference.

It all went pretty well until
that fateful day Dr. Nefarious
took Brian hostage.
Damn those villains and that thing they have
about "hurting the one you love!"
Even after I saved Brian in an extravagant,
electrifying show of power,
wit, skill, and beauty,
He still gallantly put his jacket over a puddle for me.
So sweet. So naïve.

Life after that became comfortable, nice...

...yet as weeks became months of being coddled,
catered to, and crowded over,
claustrophobia set in. I tired of coming home
to comfortable, nice, sweet, cute.
I despised doing dishes, and laundry,
and mind-numbing evenings of American Idol.
What kind of super hero enjoys a life of non-adventure?

So I dumped his sorry ass.


## Super Quiche
Madelyn Hatter

i learned normal things from comic books
like gay is great and spandex is something to fetishize
and these are normal ideas i wear on the outside
so i look like clark kent
i look like bruce wayne without the bucks
i am just an average guy in a white shirt and tie
and this is the thing that sucks
what every ordinary housewife knows that she can do
but none of us housewives can explain
when called upon for proof
the fact that we are super heroes too

sou macmillan this is a tribute poem to ladies like you
you name a son after a statue
and do more than want him to make it
you teach him to make it

by the time he is taller than the compost heap
he will have a consideration for weed whacked dandelions
that reminds you of your humanity
you named him liberty
like those kids burdened with fourth of july birthdays
and do more than want him to carry it
you teach him to carry it
the it of his middle name which is hope
not because you are waiting for it
like the person who flicks the bat signal switch
but because you are working toward it
and the organic apple pie still hits the table
promptly at six
sou your housewife magic is my super hero fix

in the company of comic book fans i was always ashamed
to say i understood spiderman's aunt may
more than superman's lois lane
my housewife identity is building a home and a family
and i have casserole cooking powers
batman could never possess
because let's face it
without alfred bruce wayne is a total mess

liberty hope macmillan is going on eight
he runs around in a bat costume
i think it's great
but there is this question of the casserole
and sou will do more than want him to cook it
she will teach him to cook it
because more than we need the bat
even more than we need the signal
we need the person who fixes the switch when it goes dead
and the person who fixes that person dinner before bed
a housewife is the farthest thing
from helpless and compliant
gotham sleeps more soundly
when citizens are self-reliant

## The Invisible Woman
Kasandra Larsen

There's a reason why you never see
Movies or Comics or Stories about me.
I'm not a singular super hero-
I've millions of sisters.
Name recognition?  Zero.
When your man leaves dirty underwear
All over the floor, and doesn't care-
When the dishes are piled from here to hell
And your guy thinks that they wash themselves,
When he doesn't see the work you do,
Paying the bills, nursing kids with flu,
You're one of us: invisible.

It isn't that unbelievable.
He can only handle one thing at a time,
While you masterfully juggle eight or nine.
Ask for him to chip in, and you've got trouble.
Somehow your "to do" list will double!
Invisible women stay silent, each day,
For they don't want love to be taken away,
So they let dear hubby think he does it all,
And they make apologies, take the fall.
Most never reveal their powers (of course).
But I did - and happily got a divorce.


## (Identity) Crisis on Infinite Earths
Jonathan Chin


It's not too difficult growing super
powers: every highschool boy has been invisible
at some point.  It's not always
the kind that slips by Dr. Doom.
In fact, for some it can hide something
as fundamental as gender
as effectively as a riveted iron mask
and emerald shapeless cape.
A teenager's X-gene for baggy pants,
and how the Chinese have only one
body type for both sexes make
for an ego-lethal combination that has people asking,
"Is that the Invisible Man
or the Invisible Woman?"

Some brothers choose to respond with lead,
not the kind The Punisher always has cocked,
nor the explosive words of Banshee,
nor the charisma of Cyclops or Havoc.
They can be more subversive than that.
Susan Storm is always drawn impossibly curved
though Jessica Alba came pretty close
when she played her in the movie.  Neither
of them are Asian but it's the same caliber
of beauty for anyone ever called mother, sister, daughter.

Some need a bigger faucet
for the river they house named Rage.
Pop culture perpetuates the Oriental Man
as a welcome mat.  Well, we snap back
because we're each a little Fantastic.
We'd throw ourselves in front of any bomb
or any arachnid just to break out in blue fur
so we can get noticed.  Our only comic book hero
had no super powers; he was a Kung-Fu master.
They tell us this is a compliment: our bodies are testaments
to human achievement; how a practiced hand,
absent of iron or adamantium,
can still fight evil.

But this only pushes us back.  We become the shadows
that surround The Dark Knight, shades of yellow
that won't be separated even into simple categories
like Man.  Woman.  Human.  Mutant.

We become the back story no one bothers to read.
(who taught The Daredevil to fight?
better: who was Shang-Chi?)

We'd throw ourselves in front of any bomb
or any arachnid just to break out
in blue fur so we can get noticed,
because when we lit ourselves on fire
and stood in the paths of tank files,
it didn't help us one bit being invisible.


## Rorschach Test
Chris Fortin

now you see me
now you see yourself
now...what is it you see now?

face like a river
patience like exposed mayonnaise
face like a river
honest like a dead dog in the gutter
face like a river
foul like a bloated dead dog in the gutter
face like a river
brutal like a blood soaked dead dog in the gutter
face like a river of sinner's blood

                                    an inky river of fire

now you see...


## Mutatis Mutandis
(Motto of the Xavier Institute for Higher Learning)
Stephen Blaiklock

Half-formed, like three-legged tadpoles in a pond,
punk-rocked, pissing like queers, we stormed against squares,
clawed at invisible force fields, squashed hulks past panel after panel
until, arriving at the smutty cover, we shrugged our Cardiff shoulders
and, collect, the dour physician began to dial.

Costumes came unglued. A few had forgotten swim trunks,
but paddled dog, metal-boned. None went home; none on buses;
but riddled with dots, Pop Art. Flimflammed, defected from our doctor,
we smudged thumbprints of hybrid feet across the pulp, stained
even to the margins with naked, mercuric surfers streaking.
Kryptonite! Radiate, spiders! - A prom night of fumbling,

overpainting Amazon bras and leopard crotches,
detaching beetle belly buttons with X-Acto knives;
but Mary Jane still was limned and hemmed and penned in,
watercolored as an Ebermensch in Miller or Moebius...
stenciled blunt as a bombshell on the nose of a B-17;
transparent as X-ray vision or green lamplight,
Peach-skinned and widowed black, I spied her drawing.
In all the graphic novels beyond my teenage reach
she tsks at me, penciling, erasing, tracing.
If in some marvelous comic book we too could out
blot the long- and latitudes you bound her in,
and harness the white thought balloons bubbling from her hair,
her vermilion hair, like a brain kept alive in a jar;
if we could prophesy, at the scene of the crime, the grapnels
come sharpening from the voluptuous utility belt,
cliched as invincibility, ridiculous as deus ex machina,
if we could ferret out the identities cowled by
animal countenance, secreted behind unbreakable Coke bottle glasses?
my Inker, you would not print, with bold block caps
for rough beasts night-schooled in alternate universes,
the old editor's Note: MUTATIS MUTANDIS,
MUTATO NOMINE.


## Clark Kent
Gregory Garofolo-Gonzalez

It's a costume,
I know.
That "S" on your chest
put an "S" on my face.
It's weird to think
your change of clothes
affected me more
than it did you.
Perhaps your cape
covered your tubes
and hoses.
I can not forget
that Halloween,
I felt I could conquer
all you desire;
blue spandex
with red,
gave me hope
that you could
fight death.
As you grew tired,
I acknowledged
your fright.
I realized-

you were Superman
without the cape or tights.

## Secret Identity
Ryler Dustin

I am the secret identity without the superman,
hiding behind words like Clark Kent's glasses,
stopping speeding trains of thought and leaping over your short attention spans.
I am a Captain Planet clubhouse still waiting to be filled with all my fans,
ravenous to replace my missing half with the adoration of the masses.
I am the secret identity without the superman.

I am alone in the light of my computer, burning words inside my trash can.
I am the frat boy with thirsty eyes, making my poetic passes,
stopping speeding trains of thought and leaping over your short attention spans.
I am my own Solomon Grundy, hatching a tragic master plan
while sparring with my nemesis Loneliness in endless, epic clashes.
I am the secret identity without the superman.
I am scribbling down my memories of El Salvador and Amsterdam,
buying your love with truths I find sifting yesterday's ashes,
stopping speeding trains of thought and leaping over your short attention spans.
I am Batman with my back against the wall,
tossing words to survive like POW or BAM,
each week waiting for you six feet deep under deceptively green grasses.
I am the secret identity without the superman,
stopping speeding trains of thought and leaping over your short attention spans.


## Blood from Stone
(for Lisa King)
Curtis Meyer

I never told Reed or anybody else.
But for the first week after the crash, I kept having these wild nightmares;
I kept reliving the moment of impact,
when the fire came in waves, seconds before I blacked-out.
I would have probably woken up in a sweat every night
if I still had my sweat-glands.

I can still remember waking up in the hospital -
Head pounding like a jackhammer,
and wouldn't'cha know it, in walked the Day.
The Universe reared its ugly head, and it was me -
staring back from the face of a mirror
like the punchline to God's biggest joke.

I spent the first few months trying to cut my wrists -
my skin was too thick to be penetrated by razors.
I couldn't hang myself because my fingers were too big
to tie knots in rope.
I could've jumped off a building, I guess,
But the worst I could do, would be to leave a crater in Times Square.

Sometimes I miss the simple things - like shaving,
or cutting my fingernails,
peeling oranges,

jokin' off.
Thinking what it'd be like to have a son or daughter.

But I've given up on all that.
Sometimes I sit back and wonder, "Is this really my life?"
I've seen it all kid,
traveled to every country you can think of -
been to outer space -
blasted through alternate dimensions.
I even died once.
Well, once that I know of,
(all these parallel timelines,
who knows what's for real anymore.)
Anyway, THAT was interesting...

But no matter where I go, not ONCE have I been able
to enjoy a quiet moment
without some bozo trying to do me in.
It'll happen again one day, I know it.
This time, for real -
no coming back.
If it's not Doctor Doom, it'll be Galactus.
If it's not Galactus, it'll be Mole-Guy,
or Rat-Face,
or Particle Man,
or maybe just some dumb schmuck
"Super-Villain of the Month" who got lucky.

There's a whole lotta death in what I do kid.
I've seen too many good folks leave too soon.
So when I crack a joke, remember,
it's to keep from crying.
When I smoke my cigars,
it's because some death feels like therapy
in the face of bigger things.
And sure, I can demolish buildings with my bare hands,
make accordions out of small cars, but
I've grown numb to signing "It's Clobberin' Time!" autographs.
Rocks erode.
Nothing lasts forever.
Dirt and sand get blown away.
That ain't me bein' deep.
I ain't no poet, that's just the truth

So if you think ya can do what I do, come and get it.
If you're eager to do the opposite, ya gotta get through me first.
Either way, I can guarantee
ya don't know what yerself getting into,
yer not ready for the pain of losing friends.
'Cause beneath the green skin and armor
we're all made of flesh and bone.

But don't cha think fer a second
Yer taking down Aunt Petunia's favorite blue-eyed nephew
Without a world full o' hurt.

'Cause I can show ya what it means to try
to get blood from stone


# The Ballad of Barry Allen
(For Carmine)
Jim Infantino

I've got time to think about the meaning of the thousand
variations of the beating of a wing of a hummingbird
suspended in the aspic of the world moving slower than
molasses as I'm off to catch the girl who is falling off the cliff
and I'm there before she knows it
I'll be gone before she sees me
with my hand around her waist
I pull her back to safety
by the time she knows what's happened
there'll be someone else who needs me
because time keeps dragging on, and on, and on, and on
(time keeps dragging on)

I've got time to think about my past as I dodge between the
bullets how my life was so exciting before I got this way and how
long ago it was now I never can explain by the clock
that's on the tower or the one that's in my brain
and I'm there before you know it
I'll be gone before you see me
and I'd like to get to know you
but you're talking much too slowly
and I know you'd really like me
but I never stick around
because time keeps dragging on, and on, and on, and on, and on

And you say the world goes rushing by
but it seems so slow to me
and you see a blur around you fly
but it takes too long
it seems so slow to me
(time keeps dragging on)

How I wish I'd never gone into my lab to experiment that night
before lightning flashed around me
and time changed speed
now I have to try to be so patient and wait for calamity to strike
because when things change in an instant
it's almost fast enough for me
and I'll be there before you know it
I'll be gone before you see me
and do you think you can imagine
anything so lonely

and I know you'd really like me
but I never stick around
because time keeps dragging on, and on, and on, and on, and on

And you say the world goes rushing by
but it seems so slow to me
complain I'm gone before you blink your eye
but it takes too long
it seems so slow
And you say the world goes rushing by
but it seems so slow to me
and I want to be there while you laugh or cry
but it takes too long
it seems so slow to me
(time keeps dragging on)
and on
and on


## The Passion of the Bat
Adam Stone

There are nights you can't sleep
because your neighbors are partying
or your roommates are fucking the walls down around you

There are nights you can't sleep because
your mattress is too lumpy
or your flight leaves early the next morning

There are nights the phone won't stop ringing
or the dreams are too vivid

There are nights you can't sleep
because you can't remember the last words
your mother said before she died

There are nights you can't sleep
because you can remember
you do remember

There are nights that you can sleep
but you won't
because every hour you sleep another crime goes unpunished
another body to the morgue

This is one of those nights
The night a craving graduates to a crusade
This is where orange meets gray and dusk is born
This is Gotham
Miles away from Metropolis
another world away from Superman
I am Bruce Wayne
altruistic millionaire with a cool car and a bat suit
But please don't call me super hero
I don't dispense justice or vengeance
Vengeance is for the weak minded

Justice is a rainbow in an oil slick
Clark Kent went blind looking for the pot of gold at the end of it

But at the end of the day
Clark sleeps
Green Lantern sleeps
But I can't
So I keep vigil until the signal goes up
safe from dreams of Dick Grayson abandoning me
to become Nightwing
and Jason Todd's explosive passion

When I feel lonely
I clutch bullets to my Kevlar vest
whisper sweet Miranda Right nothings
into unsuspecting ears

While the papers call me hero or Dark Knight
the tights and cape crew mutter "vigilante"
They invite me to their Justice League out of politeness
are shocked when I accept

They think I'm jealous of their abilities
flight, invulnerability, super speed

I'm not

Unlike them, I can claim my crusade as choice
not birthright
And I can buy gadgets to make me more powerful
than any of them

I have money like criminals have bullets
more than should be humanly possible
But never enough to sleep at night


## Batman Contemplates His Place in the Justice League
Victor Infante

Not born of planets dying beyond stars,
nor transposed from dead worlds by mad science.
Not gifted by alien light.

No monarch underneath the waves,
nor royalty from a shrouded island.

My life has not been marked by lightning,

unless the flash of gunfire itself is lightning
and the alleyways themselves are beyond stars;
this ever-lit flame an island,
reworking rage into science,
loss crashing against my chest in waves
as the bats silhouette against the light,

78

the light,
the bone-on-bone lightning
of violence in waves
beneath indifferent stars -
call this broken-heart ballet science,
this criminal oasis an island.

I think of them- the schizophrenic warrior-peace of the island,
accepting magic rings from light,
apparating like a magician's assistant through science,
bathed in chemicals and lightning.
Seeking home while staring at the stars,
or looking up from beneath the waves -

Envy soaks me in muffled waves.
They see my darkness as an island -
I am Earth where they are stars,
the shadow to their shining light.

The difference sears my skin like lightning:
They are prestidigitation. I, cold science,

and in cold science
an equation convulsive as waves,
dangerous as lightning:
This criminal math reveals an island,
and each bruised fist reveals a particle of light -
the wished-for ending under night's first stars:

That someday I'll step off of the island,
into the light;
Tranquil, for once, beneath the stars.


## The Temptation in Every Bottle
Stephen Meads

The metal is cold
around my body; the metal
is cold, protection is cold.

They all look at me. They say
they're looking to Captain America
because he's more than a man,
he's a symbol they can believe.
But when I look at them, I know.

This metal is cold.
Do they think it's easy
to be cut off from the world?
What's keeping me alive
is what alienates me
from everyone outside.

The metal is cold.
I've tried to heat it before;
an alcoholic slip of the tongue
to jump-start my heart, as though
what's frozen inside of me could melt.
Clean and sober, I still feel it.
Even when I look at Captain America,
and I know he knows
my heart is cased in metal, but
it's only the metal that's cold.

My body is jacked into a shell
and the metal allows for great things.
I have saved the world so many times,
sometimes I think about the irony-
I save lives with weapons of war.
My greatest failures
are all the things I can't fix:
like myself, like other people.

The metal is cold around my heart.
My name is Anthony Stark,
I'm an alcoholic with a shrapnel heart
and iron will.  There is only the cold
left to encase me.  This metal,
it's so cold.

## A Solemn Meditation on the Fantastic Four
Todd Swift

How can Mr. Fantastic knowingly enter the fragile
space of his own beloved, without a shameful thought:
that what simple anatomy has wrought, his husbandry
may undo, with his newfound abilities – pure expansion?
Obscenity is no part of the vows that bind a man to spouse,
but in the broken house that is radiation's special curse,
who can argue for his long-legged will to stay, just so?

And who may know the proper measure of Ben Grimm's
agony: mightier than a slaughterhouse of oxen, still stone
on stone, and tangerine, his hands a clear sign of clumsy
cold, no subtle fingers here, a demolition of thumbs, a face
like a wrecking ball, and all the passion of a normal man?
Might he not want to break down, be regular now, and take
the blind girl in his athlete's arms, again, no pressure to tackle

Victor Von Doom?  Consider the Invisible Girl, later Woman,
whose grace is to go unnoticed, who can keep the rain off
with a shrug of atoms, does she want her genius long or short;
maybe after a homely battle, she may turn her back and leave
her powers on, so no marriage can reach, no matter the arms
that struggle to strain and pound at her inviolable places?
For Johnny Storm, no tonnage of car wax or peroxide obscures

his film idol's grin eats only oxygen and spits lewd fire, his trim
physique a mitochondrion's macrocosm gone supernova.   Sure,
he's beauty jetting from a flame-thrower, a solar rose, flight hotly
incarnate, a stream of fuel lit and flown across the sky, lean muscle
in a tight blue uniform that accepts the burn... but this, and less.
Johnny cannot lift his playmates to the sun, as he himself
may go, but must return too soon with lovers to the ground.


## Under the Bridge
Nina Simon

> *In 2002, a physicist proved that Spiderman had caused his girlfriend, Gwen
> Stacy's, death in 1973 by catching her too quickly with his web after the Green Goblin
> pushed her off the side of the George Washington Bridge.*

Later, he peeled his web from her thigh,
studying the delicate grid of cuts
crossing her calf, her skin segmented
like a dark city. He traced the fault lines
that shot across her spine, square acres
as seen from airplane windows, borders
red, liquid.
There was no one else to blame:
the villain on the bridge,
the wind- all faded as her bruises
sharpened into arguments.
Her body shook like a nun's finger
unraveling a long thread of reproach
for him to tangle into years.
Her final face: stung, struck dumb.
Her winged hair floating in the air.
He cursed his hands, clutched his knees.
She sang a song only the water could hear.


## Communique from the Hornet's Nest
## The Green Hornet
Patricia Smith

Teetering on a barstool of rust and ripped canvas,
he downs something Republican from a smeared shot glass.
It's a jolt designed to slam shut the drumming systems
of a normal man. He's summarily dismissed whiskey,
never caring for the way it flirts with the heart muscle,
then shivers and retreats. Suddenly, he's developed a taste
for tiny murders of increasing voltage, inky concoctions
swirling with propane and spit. He watches the bartender
shove his salvation's square, icy hips into filigreed crystal,
cracked plastic, tonight a heavy-bottomed glass still wearing
the hard clutch of the man before him. On the juke, a dead
blue growler begs to be heard again in a voice that is
spent matches and rain-slick rock, the perfect soundtrack
for men who are men only because of the masks they wear.

He was so much huger when he slapped it on, the hard plastic
narrowing his eyes and smashing his cheekbones. Beneath it
he was still himself, only unflappable and armed. The sleek
gun hardened all of him, over-revving the ludicrous lime of
his eerily-creased sharkskin, drowning out his lack of magic
sight, his inability to soar, his stupidly human body. The cocky
fedora never wavered as he punched smoking holes into the
world's wrongs, never thinking himself vulnerable, but his skin,
dammit, was no shield. Of course he knew that someday
they would see past the mask straight into his tearing eyes,
they would realize that his spectacularly cool car needed keys.
Then he would be pointed at, filed away, left alone to ponder
the keenness of bats, the resilience of spidery limbs, steel
musculature and the allure of a past folded into the explosion
of a doomed planet. Once he was found out, they poked at
him, spat as he strode by, keyed the Black Beauty and ridiculed
his overwrought greenness, urging him to "at least fuckin' buzz."
And now this:
Accompanying John Lee Hooker in a poisonous key.
Drinking the knives he dreams of.
Ignoring the barkeep's slowly shaking head.
Hotpissing himself in a whiskey fog.
And the odd, the sad occasional, the scribbling of his useless signature
on limp cocktail napkins, wise-asses staring at a stubbled monster
in the barroom mirror. What he needed to be super was another drink,
another bomb laying waste to his throat, settling in his overlapped gut.
Then he'd damn them all and snap on the mask, conjuring those
thrill days when he dripped women and concrete buckled beneath his cock,
those days when covering his face turned him into God, those blessed days
when men were too wildly dazzled to glimpse the human in him. After all,
he had a whip hand, a loaded gun, no face to speak of. And he commanded
a pissed and whirling Chinaman who could fly and lay their asses flat.

## I Do Not Trip on My Cape
Kelley J. Cooper

sometimes i am bigger
than daddy and i
pick him up and
sometimes i am so small
mommy can't see me way back
in the closet with
the beach bag where
sand is big as rocks.
i say magic spells to
turn my sister into a
peanut butter and jelly
sandwich because i am
hungry and she also
gives me soda.
i do not trip on my cape.
i can run faster than cars
in my new sneakers and
i also walk on the

ceiling. i watch my
next door neighbor
who is a spy
whisper secrets into the
phone and he draws
treasure maps. i tell
all my stories to george
who pretends to sleep
in the sun but really
he is planning to take
over the house and eat
steaks out of the freezer.
soon i will have skates
then no one in the world-
not even superman-
will ever catch me.

## 19 July, 1997
Jessica Dalzell

Dear Francine,

You say it's funny how when you don't care if flowers last at all, they seem to live the longest. I see you finger a white rose from your grandmother's grave. It's falling apart more and more every day, but that doesn't stop you from holding it close to your breath.

On a whim, I bought you these red carnations once; they've got to be the ugliest flower, but only because they're the second most commonly bought. Carnations aren't exotic; they are for Casey or some woman at the mall. I threw them away because I realized you deserved something as rare and as hard to find as you are.

Freddie never bought you flowers; that dumb bastard. I never understand why men don't do the little things. He should have been tripping over himself doing the little things for you, Francine.

I tried again. I brought you home a silk bouquet; I didn't want you to keep loving loss. Turns out I still didn't get it right. That's when you told me they have to be real; they have to be able to die.

I know you from another time
When bubble-gum was a prince of mine,
And I'll get you alone one day
When super heroines decide to play.

Francine, it's a good life with you in it.

All my love,

Katchoo

# Henchman
Dave MacPherson

At night, when I can't sleep, I sometimes turn on Nick at Night and watch the old Batman TV show, so I can see Burt Ward kick my father's ass. There he is,

my father, dressed in an unflattering metallic gray jumpsuit and a bald cap, when he was a henchman for the Egghead. And there's Robin, all red and yellow and green, toss out an un-connecting left hook, and my father is propelled backwards into a conveniently located pile of crates. And the screen goes to bold letters:

BAM!

POW!

ZAP!

Which are the sound effects of the Dynamic Duo kicking my father's ass.

In the '60s my father was a struggling actor and part-time stuntman. Worked pretty regular for the Batman show. Henchman for the Riddler, King Tut, the Joker. He never spoke. Or acted. He just threw fake punches, wore loud clothes and looked dumb and malleable. He would be totally committed to whatever villain's plan for world domination he was contracted to that week.

He and a few other plus-sized actors always were the henchmen; they were interchangeable. I imagined a union hall for henchmen. I could see it. My father, a member of Henchmen's Local 135. Punching a clock for his shift, stopping in mid left hook for his mandatory coffee break, demanding a better health plan, one with dental. He would go into the Hall, get the assignment for the week. Pick up the new costume and do the bidding of others. Doing the job. Doing the crimes.

The truth was, my father was as successful an actor as he was a henchman. He was destined to be knocked out. And as a father, he had the same glass jaw.

Biff!

Slam!

Krack!

He left when I was seven. He didn't like the father scene. He couldn't find the right motivation. His lines always came out lifeless and flat. So off for new thrills: drugs, women, whatever. New clothes. Old crimes.

And now, I do not have any clear memories of him. I remember him mostly as the Riddler's Henchman on TV. Poorly dressed. Badly coordinated. Destined to fail. As long as there are reruns, my father's failures are eternal for everyone to witness. And I can't pull myself away from watching.

## Super Boy
Joe Fusco Jr.

He's hard to love, even like on many occasions.
He's sneaky, prone to fibs, and very aggressive with playmates.
His younger brother cuddles and kisses you goodnight,
talks in a whisper, saunters around the house
like a junior Eyore.
Joey gives you a "nod" goodnight, shouts his demands,
races around the house like Tigger on speed.
With Dustin, we're afraid he'll come home from school
with a black-eye from a bully.
With Joey, we're afraid he'll buy a rifle and get
directions to the nearest watchtower.
Who knows what's going on behind these steel-blue
eyes, that stoic demeanor. I've seen him shrug off
three vaccinations then ask the doctor for an extra lollipop.
Last night he had a seizure, body flopping around like
a minnow on a hook, eyes as huge and hollow as whoopee pies.
This morning, I gave my 8-year-old Superboy a hug and
prayed for his health. Quiet as a church-mouse, he
stayed on my lap and worried about the Kryptonite.

## 38 Pounds
Brian Comisky

I recall
it was in my bedroom
above the football game in the living room,
my sister-in-law on the phone,
my niece crying,
my mother knitting with the radio on,
I wrote.
Or has no time passed and instead I write.
Ideas stopping and starting
revisions again,
flustered by inspiration
as it touches down
only for seconds at a time
on the page.

One lone knock
but more like a thud
hits my door.
In the middle thought
I write
hoping someone is not there.
Another thud,
my doorknob turns precariously,
"Uncle Brian"
my nephew Danny
eyes up, shoulders shrugged,
he hides his hands behind him.

He's four and half and he's only been in
my room a few times.
"Uncle Brian, I drank all my milk
and ate a whole peanut butter and jelly sandwich."
I congratulate him, "That a boy, Danno."
He's small, with a terrible appetite.
I don't think he's ever finished a whole
sandwich before.
I keep telling him to eat,
to eat to get big and strong,
as I flex my biceps and he shrieks,
and drinks his milk.

I'm his favorite uncle
he tells me so all the time,
but now he's in my room
and I need to finish what I'm working on,
when he starts picking things up and asking,
"What is this? what does this do?"
and I don't want to ask him to leave,
because I've never been anyone's favorite uncle before,
but I need to finish what I'm working on,
when he walks over to my desk.
I'm sitting on my bed watching.
He is silent for moments.
He looks up over my desk,
two posters look down upon him,
T.S. Eliot
and Bruce Lee.
He fixates on Bruce Lee,
"Wow," he finally says,
"he's big and strong."
    "Yeah, he is."
"How strong is he?"
    "The strongest." I say.
"Stronger than you?"
    I nod.
"Is he your friend?"
    I nod.
"Where is he?"
    "He's dead."
There is a pause,
Danny stutters,
"Oh, he wasn't bi..bi..big and str..stro...strong enough?"
    "I guess not."
"Oh, you're gonna be bi..bi bigger and str..stro...
stronger aren't you?"
    I say, "Yes."
"You're never gonna die?"
    I say, "No."

I close what I'm working on.
I'm watching poetry first hand.

Danny, my thirty-eight pound nephew
has just made me feel so big and strong
that I
could now
cry.


## Super Heroes
Clarissa Earley

The refrigerator's empty and the house is stone cold
The mom is drunk on the couch
The father is gone and the mask has worn off
And the child is left to slouch

The carpet is burned by stains all unknown
And the electric bill hasn't been paid
And the child looks out of the window and wonders
When he can end this charade

The blue Superman flies by my door in the night
And the red Spider crawls up the wall
And the Green Lantern lit up the bloodthirsty streets
When Thing smashed open a wall
And the stars come out oh so late in the night
Only to light up this place
There's a world being created with no heroes in it
That have a familiar face

The baby cries, as his own mother dies
And the people at school do not know
That he makes his own lunch, and he makes his own bed
And he's done it ever since he was 4

The things we do to please ourselves
Without a care in our minds
We're only creating these unbreakable chains
Which put others into new binds

Even villains are here, over there, everywhere
When you've lost your sense of respect
But with no super hero  to hold you in the night
You must save your own world by yourself

And the blue Superman flies by my door in the night
And the red Spider crawls up the wall
And the Green Lantern lit up the bloodthirsty streets
When Thing smashed open a wall

And the stars come out oh so late in the night
Only to light up this place
There's a world being created with no heroes in it
That have a familiar face

## Bird-Watching in the City
Sarah Sapienza

I'm the only one that's safely within
sight now, out of bed again, but
in my mind you are always flying high:
over Gotham, Metropolis, Paradise Island.
You were bigger than them,
never needed a sign in the sky,
a phone booth, or an invisible jet to fly.

Bird-watching in the city, you'd identify birds and airplanes.
We never saw Superman up there,
not even a rope to suggest it was Batman swinging
("Stupid bastard couldn't even fly").

Instead, you looked for truth at the bottom,
always said your lasso was in your other pair of pants

when I knew you had burned it, broken it
("It can't be broken, Stupid - it's indestructible") -
ok, traded it in for something silver.

I burned the comic books:
Shit you bought when you were still in high school;
the ones we found after the flood in '96,
before we got sick, for those
train rides to your mother's house.

bruce, clark, diana:
I see nothing but pigeons,
not even any planes.


## Mutant
Sean Conlon

when I saw you last,
it was somebody's birthday party
your hair was parted to the side
you were wearing a nice new shirt
and tight jeans.
I closed my eyes.
Kitty Pride would have phased through the floor.
and had I been the Phoenix
I would have flown into space and devoured a star
instead, I begged a cigarette from somebody,
walked outside
and made my way home
feeling different
but not particularly special.

# Pussy Doctor
Samer Saliba

"Dad, what's this do?"
"That's to open the vagina so your dad can take a better look"

Can you imagine the horror? Eight years old, somewhere between my nap and the latest episode of Power Rangers, I learn what the term "gynecologist" means. I learn that women are so complicated and that their bodies are so complex that they need their own doctor. I learn that my father - a 5'6" Lebanese guy with hair everywhere except the top of his head- is what my friends later called...a Pussy Doctor.

Elementary School - "That's Sam, his dad's a doctor."
Middle School - "That's Sam, his dad's a 'Pussy Doctor'!"
High School - "That's the Pussy Doctor's son."

If there was one thing people ever knew about me, it was that my dad was a gynecologist. My teachers would ask me if I could set them up with free laser hair removal appointments, while my middle-school girlfriend dumped me because she found out her mom was my dad's patient.

Whenever my dad saw me crying and called me a pussy, I had to take his word for it.

My work experience consisted of working in a gynecologist's office at age sixteen, with forty-two women all over thirty, organizing files filled with pictures that a sixteen-year-old should never see. My dad leaves magazines lying around called "Gynecologist's Digest" and it is the most fucked-up kind of pornography in the world.

My Dad comes homes smelling of vagina, and not young vagina; nooo - *Old* Vagina. The type you have to respect, 'cause it's seen shit you can only read about in books.

But enough about the bad. How about the good? When all other boys fled when the word "period" was mentioned, I stood my ground. When my girlfriend said we couldn't "do" anything because something was wrong and she didn't know what it was, I asked if I could take a look. When something freaky happens to a woman's body, Google is my SECOND choice.

But I'm not just the son of a gynecologist, I'm the son of MY dad,

- A dad who brings sons and daughters into the world to watch their first breath; or has to tell a mother that her baby won't be taking one,

- A dad who sees the beginning of life every day as he gets older, and shares that joy with his own kids,

- A dad who treats breast cancer within his patients with the same severity as if they were his own daughters,

- A dad who stitches the head of a stillborn baby back onto its body so that its mother can hold it in her arms in one piece,

- A dad who taught me the importance of women in the world, and that taking care of them should be our first priority,

- A dad who has seen some things that men should never see, yet still goes about life with a happiness, wisdom, and sobriety that makes me, just for ONE SECOND, want to be a "Pussy Doctor" too.

Just like my dad.

## Hero
Robert Gibbs

My real life super hero came to my house today,
To get two boxes of macaroni and cheese,
a can of tuna, and some free weed.
And it's ok with me because I put away my childhood toys
a long time ago, and I know
that this man who just had his hand out
thought about me before I did at times,
so some of mine is gonna be his.
But this doesn't make a difference at times ,
because I am sick and tired
of helping my hero fly, and my eyes might mist
but I will never cry wasted tears
over some one else's wasted years again.
I guess in the end that happy is a frame of mind
that will easily turn sour
over time, if you let it and then hours
can cut like razors.
And players eventually become played out.
He stood there in his old but polished black boots jeans
with patches and stitch marks that weren't there
when they were new.
And what could I do, standing in front of a 46 year old man
with a can of tuna in his hand,
telling the same old stories.
"I'll pay you back, you'll see. I'm gonna get paid and then were gonna have it easy!"
And that's what he always said, and I know
he will do what he always did,
with the best intentions to do the right thing in the beginning. 'Cause inside,
he holds hope that this time might be different,
and that this time he might not go to that yellow house right down the block
where the password is green;
... it's an airport, if you know what I mean.
Everyday people fly away.
And I know he means well but hell,
how many 35 mm cameras 13 inch tvs, dvds,
and cds can somebody steal before you just can't feel the same way?
I have heard 6 excuses for every day
that I have been alive, and I have cried
10 times as many tears, but I am all cried out,
dried out, and time is running
out, so I gotta go.
And no, I am not abandoning you- you're my hero- but
Im just busy searching for
the pieces of myself that I let fall out of my soul
so you could keep afloat.

But right here, today, I am letting go.
So sew the holes in your cape, get some new tights
put the Kryptonite away,
and fly for me again.
'Cause sometimes we all need a hero, and this is my sometimes,
and we don't have much time. So hurry up, catch the bad guy,
put him in jail, save the train before it goes off the rails,
'cause you might not get another chance.
And fly- 'cause at some point you might not be able to stand,
and I don't plan on picking you up again,
big brother. I know you needed a father,
and I know as you got older life got harder, and
you sheltered me from a lot of the storm;
but that time is gone and we need
to move on. So listen:
in that drawer, second to the floor on the right hand side, is a costume and
if you can no longer make it fit, it doesn't matter,
'cause you can fake it,
I will believe. I promise.
So please, big brother,
go fly for me...


## X-Men & the Micronauts
Kitt Jennings

Misty rain cracks and steams off two bare neon signs
clinging to storefront, barely protected under dripping eaves.
"Games – Comics – Toys," one mutters with a yawn.
"Buy – Sell – Trade," the other commands.

In these slave hands I hold the dead weight
of all the lies learned in childhood,
the glass shard dreams that cut adults
who once hoped, and then learned better.
I await judgment at the front counter, watching as
the clerk paws through my comics, pausing
to inspect the four-part "X-Men & the Micronauts" series,
plastic-sheathed and sealed with the gravity
of adolescent blood ritual. He glances up to search
my stone face for some chiseled message
before exposing them to air for the first time
in ten years.

A hundred sun-dappled afternoons
and a hundred rain-soaked days
are folded between these pages, some scarred and scuffed
by the grasping, tearing tree trunks I used to climb
on a quest for solitude and uninterrupted reading time.
Thick boughs closed around me like a fist, immobilized me
like the broken wrench engulfed
by a gnarled knot of cottonwood
in my granddad's ancient, overgrown backyard.

Here, I learned what I needed to be:
a justice-clad avenger,
unbowed by hardship, dripping with virtue, honest, loyal,
stronger than the darkest checkered past, better than any
supposed "impossible" task, fair and
charming and clever and true,
with thirty-mile legs and an inability
to accept anything less than
the just-in-time saving of whatever it is
that most begs for saving
at that particular moment. But I should also remain human.
Deeply flawed and cracked underneath
that glossy varnish of spandex,
wisecracking and ass-kicking.
Tormented by a yearning love,
or haunted by deeds once forged in the fire of rage,
before turning onto the Path of Good and Right.

Once, I thought I had achieved this as I stood before
a towering wall of Douglas fir and flame, getting paid
to save the world. But I just drank the money.
I'm still a liar.
Tiny mistakes still kill people, and they stay dead.

The musty joy and ache of childhood still won't pay my rent.
I hear it rains for months here.


## Some Heavy Stuff
Sam Gaskin

I miss your touch
I miss her kiss
I miss

I miss-teriously was reunited with my entire childhood manifested in one Ghostbusters action figure- the one where you press the arm and his neck extends, his jaw drops, and his tie shoots out, no doubt due to setting eyes upon some effervescent fiend.

But what I remember most about this action figure specifically, is that every one of my friends who owned it as well, had broken off the tie. Mine, to this day, remains intact because I never really played with him.

Sure, I put him in various poses, had him drive the official Ghostbusters car, and pressed on his arm relentlessly; but unlike most kids, I never came up with elaborate scenarios of adventure for my toys.

I just liked to look at them, and I felt comfort knowing that I possessed them.
Hi, my name is Sam and...I have a problem, I'm a collector. I buy things that I will need in complete limited-edition sets with money I don't have. That's right, Mom, not a single one of those checks ever went to the PTA.

It's worse than being a junkie, at least a junkie's habit eventually kills them. For me, there's always a new issue, a reissue, a remix, a never-before-seen ending, and exclusive behind-the-scenes footage that feeds into my veins and keeps my heart beating as I spend sleepless nights, bagging and boarding, BAGGING AND BOARDING, comics that will never go up in monetary value because even after thirty years, no one knows who Harvey Pekar is.  What's in a name?

Who is Sam Gaskin?

Is he manifested by all this people-shaped plastic that sits on the shelf and collects dust? Or is he the dust itself that is sent into a swirling frenzy by one quick blow from pursed lips?

I miss her
I miss-teriously found myself lost in my backyard after
I miss-takenly broke off Egon's tie.
My clumsy adult fingers were trying to make up for lost time.


## Crazy Leap of Faith
Ryk McIntyre

You know the sound a straightjacket makes
when the safety-straps slip?   Baby,
that was our first kiss!
We knew it'd be crazy, knew the risk -

to get involved like this,
we'd have to disagree to agree
with the voices in our heads
that sentence us to solitary,
and do something really crazy,
like...not listen to them!
Set ourselves loose enough
to measure the space
it takes to live happy,
with one last leap of faith.

Fortunately, you've got good, strong legs for jumping,
and I'm pretty sure my brain is a helicopter.  We can do this.

Too many people zone themselves off
for their own protection.
Building lives according to blueprints for misery,
becoming Monuments To Alone, when they don't have to be.
There is always somewhere beyond our tenuously held borders,
where the rooftops reach out with the same promise the sky makes to fledgelings:

"You can go anywhere in the world you want,
all you have to do is trust in something you can't see or touch,
and jump.  It only sounds difficult if you get weighed down in whether it's possible."
We've both had some bad falls; there's no shame there.
So even after I take the leap, you're scared.  Still stuck back there,
on your rooftop, saying, "I love you, but I don't dare.
I can't get hurt again. You better go on without me..."

Baby, I'd be crazy to leave you.  And
I'm crazy now.  So if I go,

two crazies cancel each other out and I'd be left sane.
And if I end up sane, just watch-
I'll. Go. Fucking. Crazy.

I've got a better idea -
I've got a flashlight in my pocket,
and a joke I stole from a Batman comic,
I studied physics by watching Bugs Bunny cartoons- this can work:
I'm going to turn the flashlight on,
and place it at the roof's edge...
don't you see?
You can just walk across the light beam!

And you say, "Whoa!!!
I may be crazy,
but I'm not stupid...
...you'll just turn the flashlight off when I'm halfway there!"

And I say "No. Baby, I may be crazy,
but it's not Bad-Crazy,
and the healthiest diagnosis I ever got, was: I have you.
Love isn't a cure in itself, but it can be our Invisible Friend.
It's got soft walls to bounce off,
it's our best medicine. Love can jump buildings.

Standing here today,
maybe we're both "twenty-five cents short of a dime,"
but we are fully invested in this crazy leap of faith called "us."
Our dreams have fallen short long enough.
And I understand - you need to hear the word "promise."

I promise.

If the jump scares you,
because the distance wears you down, like the meds,
just borrow my whirlybird brain and fly across,
that way you'll know that I'm committed too.
Give up if you have to; I won't give up on you.
I won't let you fall, not when a whole new city is possible for us.
And if the bad-crazy train is coming to town town?
Fuck it- let's get on the bus.

Trust me.
Jump.

I'll catch you --that's why this straightjacket has such long sleeves.
You won't believe the view, once you get over your fear.
I swear...

You can see our house from here...

# Box of Comics
Laura Vookles

The box is sitting in the hall closet. I see it every time I open that side- a whole file box full of comic books that belonged to my husband. I looked through it quickly after he died to verify the contents and see if it were something his teenage neph- ews might want. But they seemed to be mostly for adults, and I suspected some might be porn. I wondered if they might be worth some money, but I couldn't sell them before I inventoried them.

That was two years ago.

I'm always thinking I'm going to do something with that box, but it only takes up two cubic feet. Less, really. It's not much trouble. And I still don't know what's in them. But when someone dies, and you go through all their stuff, it makes you think someday you're going to die, and someone's going to go through all your stuff. Then my son will be left going through this box of comic books, and, depending on what's in them, is that really the legacy I want? So the box is always in the back of my mind. Last year, I clipped an article out of the Antiques and Arts Weekly about a vintage comics dealer, but lately I've been thinking eBay. So I've got a vague plan--it's just not high priority.

Then I'm up in Worcester, and Ryk McIntyre is looking for stories about comic book heroes. Later, it's still on my mind, and I remember, I have a whole box of comic books. That I need to do something with. I might as well write a story about them. I'm not sure what, but at least this new twist is the push I need to inventory them.

I have them all out on the bed and I'm forming stacks, sorting by series. They are all for adults, some of them say "mature content." I have 3 Black Kiss, 4 Megaton Man, 5 American Flagg, 7 Star Reach, 10 Mister X, and at least 14 Aztec Ace. Several I just find one of, like Void Indigo, Samuree, Blue Bird, Hot Stuf', Scorpio Rose, and Chaos, Princess of Madness. The titles are split about halfway between salacious fantasy and reprints of classics like Charlie Chan and Sherlock Holmes, but some of these look racy too. A few do look like they might be porno- graphic. None of this surprises me. I smile. More than 20 piles, and I'm running out of space. I grab the steno and start listing.

By my fourth handwritten page, I'm starting to consider, which ones will I take the time to read? My motives are muddled. Reconnection? Story ideas? Entertain- ment? I stop and flip through some, especially the ones with the sexiest covers. And I do find one very large, erect penis and one crotch shot, the latter in Superbitch, but other than that, they're really not porn, merely suggestive. I pick up Nightveil. There are two of these. She has a V-neckbody suit plunging to a quad D cup and rectangular cutouts in the thighs of her tights, giving a garter effect. But the intro says her secret real name is the same as mine, Laura, and she's even older than I am. She lives in a Victorian man- sion, like the one where I work, which she magically suspends above a Florida swamp. Plus, she has lots of other supernatural powers, including a cape lined with stars that my Nintendo savvy son would call a "portal." Sounds promising.

There are over 200, and I can't help asking (because I work in a museum), what are these comic books telling me? The ones that he has a lot of, like the 26 Airboys- does that mean he liked them best? In fact, I'm wondering if he really read them all, or just liked to look at the pictures. Was it just the titillation? Was it a drug thing? And I'm forming hypotheses about the years that he collected them. Most are after 1981, when he got divorced and moved down to Yonkers to work at the museum. Did he purchase his first one because he was bored and lonely? But a few, like Nightveil, date from ear- lier. Had he owned more? Why bring just these to Yonkers? Or was he buying them used, as collectibles? I guess this because a bunch are in plastic sleeves with price tags higher than what's printed on the covers. I pull one out to check the date. I realize I don't know if he ever took it out. Maybe he never even opened it. Maybe I'm the first person to do that.

Later, sorting the typed list, I see that he stopped collecting in 1989, and there's only one issue from November, the month we started seeing each other. A Sherlock Holmes. I want to think that maybe I replaced a few of those buxom babes but I'm an A-cup. More likely, it was Sam Spade, Lew Archer and all the other hard-boiled detectives he read when we were dating. I have two more boxes of those vintage paperbacks, and most of his last year of comics are mysteries, too. He'd stopped doing drugs. I don't discount that. I'm looking for anything.

I Google some titles to see if any are valuable and find another clue. I retrieve several hits, sometimes whole articles, on almost every one I try. It seems that the 1980s were peak years for these comics. Independent publishers like Pacific and Eclipse were printing countless series faster than the artists and writers could keep up. But Pacific went out of business in 1982, Eclipse in 1989. So maybe he just stopped because they did. Despite this cyber renown, I also see a whole set of Aztec Ace on eBay only bid up to $2.95. Selling might be more trouble than it's worth.

It's very late and tomorrow is a workday. I start packing the sorted comics back in the box, setting aside about 10 to keep on top. If I read them I might get an idea for a story, but I'm not so sure the real tale isn't why I still have this box of comic books. Why do you hang on to so much stuff when someone's gone? Can it make them seem closer? I'll never even know exactly why he saved them. Did he regard them as collectibles or just forget them? And I'm forlorn looking at the box and my list and the Internet printouts and thinking, they really don't teach me anything about him that I didn't already know. They're not a way that I can understand him any better than I already do. Sleep tugs at the edges of my imagination, and I see myself as Nightveil--his Nightveil. Sometimes fantasy can take you places when the facts get stuck. I enfold his memory in my cape of stars, thinking that tomorrow I'll start by reading that one.

# On Lisa King - Remembering a Heroic Life

# (Excerpt from) A Sore Loser

In the early nineties after Queer Nation had imploded a few of us ex-activists still had the itch (which some might call a compulsion) to make the world more to our liking one small, crappy bar at a time. A couple of us, along with some art school grads, started "Fishnet," a night for queer women who'd never had the inclination to listen to Holly Near.

Our spoken-word open mike, we decided, would be nothing like the one at the Jamaica Plain women's bookstore where I had witnessed one annoying woman, request before she read, "I need a hug!" And a mad rush of women had nearly knocked each other over to put their arms around her. We wanted our dykespace to be hug-free.

I went into that first Fishnet reading hating most poetry. I had a special disdain for poetry read or recited aloud. But one poet that night shouted, "Bring them back!" about all those who had died of AIDS, "...Bring back Liberace!/ So he can shove a crystal/Candelabrum up George Bush's ass." (We were in the era of George Bush I.) She was the only person I'd heard or read who could put all the rage, power, and unlikely humor of that era's queer political life into words.

I'd taken care of people in the last stages of AIDS and later read their obituaries. I'd gone to Kennebunkport to be in a massive ACT-UP die-in where I had helped burn George Bush (The First) in effigy. I'd always pushed my fellow activists to ask for more than they thought they could get, a trick borrowed from my mother, the landlord. But unlike my mother, we still got very little of what we wanted. This poet showed me that unlike activists, with our cries for prevention and treatment, artists could ask for all those lost lives back, which was impossible and unreasonable and the only fair request. I thought, "I want to do something like that." I memorized the poet's name: Lisa King.

**Ren Jender** is a writer/performer and has been published in *Bitch Magazine*, *Bay Windows* and *Spare Change*. Host and founder of The Amazon Slam (for women poetry slammers), she co-curated and co-produced the Lisa King Memorial, May 2006.

Lisa King was one of the bravest poets around! She knew that a cutting sense of humor is always your best weapon against the bullshitters and the bullshit they try to get away with. All poets, slam and otherwise, should learn from THE KING!

**Shappy Seasholtz** is the NYC-URBANA Slam-master and self-proclaimed Nerd Poet.

## On Lisa:

I knew her, sure - she was all over the scene, handsome swagger yet somehow modest - a flirt of unusual subtle grace and firm eye - the King. I admired from a place of a new poet, a new slammer, a new woman looking at other women with eyes open to see their inner qualities of heart and mind, maybe love... But I finally connected to Lisa King in a more real way one night in the early 1990's. It was at our weekly gathering of freaks, geeks, queers & queens, bikers, kings, house painting poets, poetry fans, and amused barflies - the Cantab Lounge Poetry Slam. I was performing a piece about Ronald Reagan's affect on school funding and shouted out a line or two... "CALIFORNIA...UBER ALLES..."

Lisa turned with slight jaw drop and a knowing nod - see, I'd been more known for my hiphop tributes to the heroes of the hood. We didn't know we had some Punk rock in common. Over beers we talked about the Clash (yes'm, I still consider em the only band that truly matters. The Dead Milkmen (I'd seen em at The Rat)... Patti, the Gits, the GoGo's, the Ramones. She laughed as I sang out

"..this is BOSTON/..NOT L.A.!/...BOSTON!..NOT L.A.!..BOSTON!.. NOT L.A.!... this is BOSTON, so FUCK L.A.!" laughing, so sweet. POETRY forever. I love you, Lisa.

**Amatul Hannan** is a 1990's vet of the Boston Poetry Scene, youth organizer, proudly queer sistergrrl, and costumer.

## Star Doll
to l.k.

Blink some more,
warrior woman,
voice of the underdog.
Bark toward the stars,
and turn them inside out!

Bark back from the stars toward us.
I swear I saw you wink last night: watch this!
as you sidled up to beautiful Aurora
at Sirius' corner bar.
And there was the lift of your chin,
that dimple, that impish grin.

**C. A. Coley** is a recent transplant from liberal metro-Boston to the Virginia Peninsula, where she's taken to hanging out with rocket scientists. This greatly enhances research for her young reader novel currently in progress. She is also Kenny McIntyre's mother.

        I remember Lisa best on stage. A variety of stages, actually- Berbotti's Pan in Portland, Oregon, a bar on the Cape, the Boston Public Library auditorium, the Amazon Slam at Riles in Cambridge, the Met in Providence? But I keep coming back to the Cantab. Here's Lisa behind the red chain-link that surrounds the stage, her head and shoulders rising above the fence, wearing a striped shirt under her black motorcycle jacket. Her right arm is up in description of an image in her poem, and she's squinting a little through her glasses like she's trying to decide which detail to tell the audience first. Brian Comisky is around somewhere in the room, maybe over by the bar, getting a beer from Judy, but watching at the same time. Patricia Smith is at the side of the stage, uh-huh-ing her emotions all right there on her face for anyone to read. Michael Brown is nodding, listening even with his nose down in the slam scores. Michael Holly and Jeff Paris are here too, because why wouldn't they be- it's about 1997, or 1998, it's cold out with early spring, and we've been into Nationals season a few months now already. I can smell cigarettes. Are we smoking in the bar? Is it still allowed, or has it been banned already? We're all riveted. 'Cos this is riveting stuff she's saying- it's political, and it's feminist, and it's queer & out . It's Important work, and it's Smart work, and she's going to mention the Ramones, just you wait.
        The words. Isn't everything a circumstance for poetry? It's the words that remind us of each other. The words insist, haunt us, if you will; they don't beg us not to forget, they make sure we don't. They stick out their warm, pointy noses and goose us when they think no one's looking: oft-repeated tasks elicit quotes, the same ones every time. Here is Lisa's voice, out of nowhere- tomboyish, tree-climbing, leather jacket wearing, questioning, always questioning- climbing up to whisper in my ear. I should expect it by now, really. Every butter knife pulled from the dish rack draws forth the image of doll parts. Every twenty-eight days finds me in grocery aisles, muttering under

my breath, "I don't need feminine protection" men do." For each windswept morning there is, "throw open the all windows in the worst weather / let nature take its course."

I remember: That poetry movie, the crowd and the camera, where Lisa's vamping her tattoos for Bob Holman ("If my tattoos could talk"). An Arlington living room, P-Funk is playing, people are dancing, and Lisa is laughing to someone's joke ("That's what you think!") A game of pool in Provincetown, the jukebox Lisa threw quarters into belting out Joan Jett ("Man, I love this song!") A sunny and cold afternoon in Cambridge at the copy shop, running off issues of Omnivore, off the page counter and on the clock- and on the good, heavy paper, too ("Let's do it right.") A hotel in Oregon, everyone jumps into the pool, some of us with our clothes on, even, and Lisa still wearing her glasses when she hits the water. She's laughing, grinning ear to ear, soaked and apple-cheeked, and all full of words.

**Sou MacMillan**, formerly the voice behind Caroline/Double Deuce band Pet Ufo, is currently a one-woman circus living in Worcester, MA. Look for her books - *Shallow Empire* and *Chrysanthemum* - for the full scoop...and rabbit hats.

I remember hearing people talk about Lisa after she had move to New York from Boston. Lesbians would get all goofy eyed and dreamy at the mention of her name. Everyone said how amazing she was and how much I would like her work. It was in 1999, at the Queer Slam that I first heard her- I was blown away. Everything that I heard paled in comparison. She took over the stage and had the audience before she even started to speak. I felt an instant connection to her work, as I am sure others did.

Lisa was a great inspiration to me in the honesty of her work. After hearing her and seeing her perform, it made me want to write better, say it better and mean it more. The one thing that I felt was that she really meant what she wrote. I hate regrets but I do regret not having the chance to hear more of her work and that she left this fucked up world WAY before her time.

**Zilla McCue** is a poet from Cambridge, MA and occasionally New York City.

# Our Hearts Hushed and Bleeding
## by Lisa King

There are some moments in life that are forever crystallized in
your heart.

Like that time when teetering down the sidewalk on a new bicycle
your stomach flipped with each turn of your feet.
You felt the hot waxy skin of a single tear break on your cheek
as you realized YOU were doing it.
You were riding, you were flying!
And you didn't need to look behind to see if  someone
was running along to catch you.
You didn't even look to see if they were watching,
because this was your moment.

Or when you got your first apartment.
You remember that dump you thought was a palace.
And so what if the toilet didn't work so good,
and the walls were so thin you could almost see

that woman smack her kids.
None of that would ever change the feeling you got
as you walked around for the first time in that empty apartment,
still stinking slightly of fresh paint,
and thought to yourself, it's mine.

How about that time in a bookstore
when you opened a book of poetry and found yourself
so entirely inside the lines that each word
was your own face staring back at you.
And you didn't know what to do cause nobody,
nobody had ever opened you up like that before.
And when you went to the counter to pay for it
you felt embarrassed like you were buying a porno mag
with YOUR OWN NAKED BODY on the cover.

One that will go to dust with me will be that time
in a small club, pressed sweaty and throbbing
against 200 other people at the foot of the Rock & Roll altar.
Worshipping the rock Goddess of pure kick ass fun.
The woman who kicked the shit out of tradition.
The woman who didn't give a damn 'bout her bad reputation.
And there I was, close enough to read her fucking set list.
Caught in the ripped black fishnet of raw Rock&Roll energy.
Thinking it doesn't get any better than this.  And then it did.

She shook her head, shook that shag and IT happened.
One sweet sparkling drop of Rock&Roll sweat, St. Joan sweat,
Joan Jett sweat, hit me on the right side of my bottom lip.
One moment frozen in time, MINE, just MINE!

There is no way to totally explain these moments to anyone.
We live them exclusively.
Our hearts hushed and bleeding, as the drops crystallize.
This is what we take with us when we go.
These moments of silent poetry that make up all of our lives.

# About Our Contributors

**Eric "Zork" Allen** is so super at leaping chairs in single squats that even Davy Jones (a Monkee) blurbed his book. Zork can be stalked and/or serenaded at www.stolensnapshots.com/**Sylvia Bagaglio** has been creating scribbles, doodles, and masterpieces since she was old enough to bang a hammer. At night she becomes "Tech-Rat." She is happily married to "UberMensch"/ **Kevin Bernazzani** is a student at Stonehill College/ **Jill Binder** is the Canadian of the collection. When she is not busy she flies around at night looking for evil to fight (more at jillbinder.com)/ **Stephen N. Blaiklock** manages a small department in a university library. After dark, however, he becomes the "The Lone Arranger./ **Rich Boucher** is a mild-mannered working class dog by day, by night he becomes The Invincible Crooner, with the power to mangle any song with Karaoke of Doom!/ **Stacie Boschma** is a poet living in Atlanta, GA. She was dubbed "Death of Fun" by her friends, She continues to wage pitched battles against a variety of things, and has lots of fun in the process./ **Michael R. Brown**, (the Blue Dragon ) is a Professor of Communications at Mount Ida College, author of four books of poetry, and founding Boston slam master./ **Tony Brown**? He's the big guy on the left. As "Lazor Sloth, aka Mundane Man" he uses superpowers to do the most incredibly mundane things, because hey, why waste energy?/ Wonder Woman is really **Jaime Burgess**, an aspiring super hero of love who published her first poem titled Dove in 1989 at the age of 12 in an anthology Windows of the World. She was the youngest poet in that book./ **Trevor Byrne-Smith**, better known as Captain Neurotic, has been on two Providence Poetry Slam and one Youth Poetry Slam team. He is gifted with the power to blow things up by grinding his teeth./ **James "J*me" Caroline** is a rare metamorph and deadly assassin. The top of his tongue is smooth, but the underside is a microplane of razor blades, necessitating all his assassinations be of an intimate nature. His services are not available for hire./ **Dennis Caswell** lives near Seattle and works in the aviation industry. At risk of compromising his secret identity, he has included himself in his poem- he's the Man of Feathers. At least, that's what he wants you to believe./ **Tod Caviness** discovered he could change the color of small bodies of water. As the titanic "T-Bag", he fights for some goddamn peace and quiet in the hot tubs of Orlando./ **Jonathan Chin** attends Boston University. His kryptonite include girls with cherry lip balm, mortgage annuity, actual kryptonite, and other rare earth metals./ **Brian Comisky** is a big man, but he moves like a cat./ **Sean Conlon** is a poet attending Hampshire College. As a super villain, he can alter probability; rarely used in his favor, although he does get away with an amazing amount of gossip and food theft./ **Kelly J. Cooper** is a recognized level of intelligence gone awry. She writes a column for www.Comixpedia.com called "The Webcomic Reader."/ **Pat Cosentino** is an award-winning poet, as well as Ryk McIntyre's first writing teacher. Someone should look into that./ **Kevin Coval** lives in Chicago near his father who is a super hero, "Danny Dog Walker, the canine super hero, able to walk your dog while you labor in the office for a mere $13/day./ When he is not warily circling mechanics whose physique and skin pallor are eerily like that of "The Spectre," **Tom Daley** teaches poetry. Contact him at tom.daley2@verizon.net/**Jessica Dalzell** is a transplanted Worcesterite making her new home in Albuquerque, NM. She is convinced New Mexico drivers will send her to heaven one day. Her super hero name is "The Flying J."/ **Christian Drake** had aspirations of becoming a comic book inker before deciding that comic art was a dead-end with no money in it; now he's a slam poet. He lives in Oakland and still hides issues of *Daredevil* inside the artsy-fartsy Chris Ware tomes he's pretending to read. His superpower is the same as Ant-Man's, but for brine shrimp./ **Robert Dunn** is the author of Zen Yentas in Bondage, Horse Latitudes, and Baffled in Baloneyville. Not really a super hero per se, Mr. Dunn's main power seems to be the ability to get out of bed every morning within an hour of the alarm going off./**Ryler Dustin** lives in Seattle. He has the ability to make the deaf listen when he reads./ **Clarissa Earley** aka "Twister Blister", is a single mom to a mini male cyclone "Meso-Mike". Together they cause mass chaos and destruction among the streets./ **Ry Eff** is more mysterious than some poets, less obscure than others./

Aaron Enskat has been a member of Team Normal 2000 & 2004, and Team Oakland 2005 (which finished in ninth place). He's the natural red head in the Captain Underpants T-Shirt. He has toured all three coasts, uses the word 'he' way too much, is a certified Reverend, and is down with the sickness./ **Christopher J. Fortin** has been writing and performing poetry for over fifteen years. he has also been reading comic books for much longer than that. Chris likes a hot cup of tea and a good anti-hero./ **Ed Fuqua** is also known as Edward the Melancholy, and has stories about a porpoise you may not want to hear./ **Joe Fusco Jr.** likes to write funny poems, eat, and screw. His super-hero name is Mr. Endurance. He has no powers just an irritably constant outlook on life./ **Jeannine Hall Gailey** (alias: The Masked Persona) recently published a book of poems on female super heroes and villainesses called Becoming the Villainess, from Steel Toe Books. Superpowers still under investigation, but may include speed reading./ When she's not threatening to destroy the world, **Amanda Gannon** undermines society by writing erotica, painting, and watching cartoons. Minions can keep abreast of her evil schemes at http://naamah-darling.livejournal.com/ **Karen Garabrant** is an Atlanta poet. It's possible her power is to make the Moon very, very moonlike./ **Gregory Garofolo-Gonzalez** ia Worcester-area student./ **Samuel C. Gaskin** is the Green Ghost. He knows all secrets of men and eats slime. It is kind of gross./ Len Germinara has been a venue facilitator (PoHo) for the last five years. He has co-edited, with his wife Sarah Oktay, five poetry anthologies. Known as "LMR", he has the power to start every conversation with a question instead of a statement./ Bobbie Gibbs was Worcester's rep in IWPS 2006 and has a bigger heart than he lets on./ **Bruce Gordon** lives in Seattle and has "fabulous vision". No you can't find out what that means./ **Daphne Gottlieb**'s superpower is, when not wrangling her words into books to get to press, convincing people to do ridiculous and delightful things with her, like pillow fight in leather bars./ **Melissa Guillet**...able to teach 800 children and write poetry in a single bound/ **Leigh Harrison** is the author of many books as well as an award-winning singer/songwriter. She had an on-line game super hero but can't remember what it was/ **Dr. Madelyn Hatter** is the devious and charming super hero alter ego of Chicagoan megan volpert and her super powers are witty left-wing banter and moderately obnoxious shenanigans./During the day, **Matt Hopewell** is a coffee slingin' cowboy at a cafe, but underneath the Stetson hat he has the ability to bend reality itself... he is... BipolarMan!/ **Joanna Hoffman** is also known as Super Jew Girl, and hails from the utopian wonderland of Washington, DC. Her superpowers include mind-reading, ass-kicking, and turning bad guys into matzoh balls./ **Victor D. Infante** is an award-winning writer and editor living in Worcester, Mass. His superpowers include multi-tasking and "the prickly editor's eye of death." He has no super hero name, and believes wholeheartedly that "the ones in spandex die first."/ **Jim Infantino** is a singer songwriter based in Boston. His band, Jim's Big Ego has been performing here and around the world for 10+ years and is instrumental in defining the UnPop genre of modern music. Jim lives at home with his wife and cats, cursing the world he loves. His super power is his ability to bend any subject matter in towards himself. At night he becomes "the Singularity"/ **Kitt Jennings** is Lady Anisychia's mild-mannered alter-ego. By day, she is this college student from Texas; by night, a brash and sharp-tongued warrior fighting crime wherever it hides. Her superpowers include talking smack, getting into trouble, and finding a new job every five months./ **David Keali'i** a.k.a. Arctic Boy mainly operates out of Western Mass. He first realized he had a crush on the mutant Logan when he was about 11 or 12. He can control icy arctic blasts and may or may not have bases of operations in certain Pacific Islands such as the Society Islands, Anuta, and American Samoa./ **Amanda Kail** has performed with Sister Spit and co-hosted the 'Cliterati', the South's most notorious all-Grrl poetry collective. You don't get more super than that./ **Mareh Labenski** spends her days busy, but when economic trouble's afoot, she rushes to the nearest ATM and transforms into Psychic Economy Girl. Among her powers, her best is being able to predict the rising and falling of gas prices and the widening pay gap between men and women./ **Kasandra Larsen** lives in New Orleans. Her poetry has recently appeared in "Babylon Burning: 9/11 Five Years On". She can make a pint of ice cream disappear into thin air. She also reads minds./ **Valerie Lawson**'s super hero name is "The Well-Adjusted Poet." She has a super power but she ain't tellin'./ **Alvin Lau** is a Chicago native and writer of poetry and prose. He moonlights as the super villain "IHateYourGuts" (one word), and has the ability to make supernaturally terrible grimaces in his foe's direction./ The super hero Cap'N Mack'N has the incredible power of having everyone value his opinion. Unfortunately, as mild-mannered **Rich Mackin**, his main power is talking too much./ **Dave MacPherson** is a poet and story teller in the Worcester area. He has the power to inspire./ **Jen Mahon** lives in Austin, Texas and combines martial arts and poetry in one hot package./ **Robert "Ducky" McAuslan**, the fata buena (the good fairy) battles daily to make the world a little queerer so fairies everywhere know they have a place in it./ Standup poetry guy **Jack McCarthy** is a legend in his own mind. He's been in jail, but can explain. As "What-the-Fuck-Man", he have the power to make people say, within three minutes, "What the fuck is he talking about?"/ **"Mighty" Mike McGee** is a stand-up poet living on the West Coast. He performs often because he likes people. He has the ability to tell people what mood they're in. You should check him out online./ **Ryk McIntyre** is a poet and actor. He is also Pope Noir the First, Self-Appointed Unitarian Pontiff./ **Ray McNiece** is a writer, performer, and teacher the world over. He has the power of reaching out./ **Stephen Meads**, the "Non-Sequitor Kid" has a habit of saying things that have no relation to each other. He currently lives in San Francisco where he attends SF State and watches movies for school./ **Curtis Meyer** of Winter Park, Florida was bitten by a radioactive chihuahua, and woke up the next morning to find he could steal genius from Tod Caviness as pass it off as his own. As one-fourth of Spoken Word powerhouse Quarantine Unit, he continues to fight the good fight ./ **Frank Miller** is the host of The Brockton Library Poetry series and has the power to wither by comment or glance alone./ **Chris O'Carroll** is a writer, actor, comedian, Pushcart Prize nominee, and two-time Cambridge Poetry Award recipient. If he wore a diamond shape eye mask and dyed his hair blonde, you"d swear he was Green Arrow./ **John Powers** is already a super hero name and his super hero power is to speak at the speed of sound. He is the chief curator of GotPoetry.com. John is a loving husband and father./ **Adriana E. Ramirez**, also known as Adri Monster, promises always to use her superpowers for good. She has performed poetry on stages all over the freaking country. She has a deep love of sparkling water./ **Ratpack Slim** is the alter ego of one Rob Sturma. He hosts the Los Angeles open mic Green every Monday with DJ Jedi (Digable Planets) and Joshua Silverstein (Declare Yourself). His special power should be stretching but really it's making marinated chicken on his Foreman Grill./ **Samer Saliba**, is a student at Boston University studying architecture. His power is his love for his Dad./ **Sarah Sapienza** is a poet making due in Vermont. Her super powers consist of death glares, sarcasm, and charm (just ask her mother). She thinks that shirt looks really, really great on you./ **The Klute** is the alter-ego of mild-mannered Arizona slam poet Bernard Schober. He uses the power of procrastination to not exactly stop evil, but rather, just delay it from happening. He's a card carrying member of the Guild of Calamitous Intent./ **Stefan Sencerz** is the Zen-Master. Haiku are his place of power./**Nina Simon** is a museum exhibit designer, engineer, and poet. She takes OFF her cape as the Not-So-Stealthy-Nudist, famous for quick stripping and naked appearances. Nina hangs her birthday suit in Santa Cruz, CA./ **Patricia Smith** ("The Rumbler") is the author of four books of poetry; the latest, "Teahouse of the Almighty," was a 2005 National Poetry Series winner. She's also a grandmother, a lover of purple, an MFA candidate, a cow collector and a former Slam junkie. She has the power to initiate soul-numbing orgasms at will. This doesn't prevent much crime, but it's fun./ **Morris Stegosaurus** has appeared on HBO's Def Poetry Jam, on his way to conquering the world. To watch him perform is to know his super power./When not using his Stance of Awkwardness to cripple the conversations of his enemies, **Adam Stone** dispenses coffee to overworked doctors and radiologists. He reminds readers that e-mail spammers are the real super heroes, that's why they can't divulge their identities./ **Steve Subrizi** is known to the crime world as Dr. Jumbles. He believes that this relates in some way to the popular newspaper word game. He can play such games with fair skill./ **David R. Surette**'s first book of poetry is *Young Gentlemen's School Koenisha*, 2004). He co-hosts Poetribe, a poetry series in southeastern Massachusetts./ **Laura Swearingen-Steadwell** has the superpower of kicking your ass with intelligence. It doesn't matter if she's on the west coast, she can do it from there./**Todd Swift** is a Canadian-born poet based in London. His poems have been published in *The Guardian, Poetry Review, Jacket, New American Writing* and many other journals. He has been Oxfam's Poet-in-residence since 2002, and recently edited the poetry CD *Life Lines: Poets for Oxfam.*/ **Cecelia Tan** is the editor of *Circlet Press*. Unlike most heroes and villains, she knows how to wear leather and make it look good./ **Robbie Q. Telfer** is the most important figure in spoken word today, for not only has he appeared in print SEVERAL times, but he is also the slam master at the world-famous Normal Poetry Slam. He is currently a part of the Speak Easy Poetry Ensemble in Chicago, under the direction of Marc Smith. His super hero name is "Hyperbole Boy" and he wields the power of overstatement./ **A.C. Valdez** walks by night with the moniker of "That Super Hero Dude Whose Name Is Somehow All-Encompassingly Amazing, Awesome, and Striking...Man." He's currently at work as the sole producer for www.storiesforlunch.com./ **Laura Vookles** is a museum curator and author, but in her super hero life as LV, is also a mother, memoirist and poet. LV has Spiderman hanging from her purse and dashboard, but that is just a crush./ **Andrew Watt** can write in form, or he can improv, but he can't do both at the same time. He lives in northeastern Connecticut where he works within his secret identity as a middle school teacher./ **Mike Whalen** was a member of Team Austin Ego's in 2005 and was the coach of the first-year Team Austin NeoSoul in 2006, which ranked second in the nation. His super villain name is BigSleep666, emboldened with the power to be surly./ **Beverly Wilkinson** is a mild-mannered keyboard jockey by day and a sassy word-slinger by night. Her superpower is being able to incite guilt and remorse with a single cold-eyed stare. Her super hero name is Virgo Dame but she is rethinking it because she doesn't like the logo./ **Scott Woods** is the president of Poetry Slam, Inc., runs an open mic in Columbus, Ohio and fights crime under the nom de plume "Smart Black Guy." His primary power remains unknown, but it's definitely black power.

# Acknowledgments

None of this could've been done without the following people - Melissa Guillet for having founded Sacred Fools Press and trusting me to play nice in it; to all the contributors, without whom, we would have NOTHIN'; to the Estate of Lisa King for their enthusiasm and encouragement for this project; all the people that spread the word and offer support still - that's how we make communities; and to comic books and heroes and the belief in better things.

Many of the poets sent much bigger bios that had to be trimmed for the sake of space. For further information on the contributors or their work, send inquiries to **theryk@yahoo.com** and they will be forwarded appropriately. Likewise many of these poems appeared previously in self-published chapbooks, and if you like what you read and want to buy a book by one of the poets, let us know; we'll forward those inquiries too. Officially: "Stan Jablonski-Zombie Hunter" was previously published in "My Favorite Bullet" and "Psycho Moto Zine"; "Legion Of Doom" appears courtesy of Soft Skull Press, and was originally published in *Why Things Burn* (2001); "The Ballad Of Barry Allen" is reprinted with permission from the writer and originally appeared as a track on the Jim's Big Ego album, "They're Everywhere" © 2005 Jim's Big Ego, published by Funny/Not Funny Music (ASCAP) Some rights reserved; a different version of "A Solemn Meditation on the FF" was originally published in *Budavox,* 1999; "Our Hearts Hushed And Bleeding" appears by kind permission of the Estate of Lisa King.

www.ingramcontent.com/pod-product-compliance
Lightning Source LLC
Chambersburg PA
CBHW051835040426
42447CB00006B/534